THE FEMALE BRAND

THE FEMALE BRAND

USING THE FEMALE MINDSET
TO SUCCEED IN BUSINESS

Catherine Kaputa

Davies-Black
an imprint of Nicholas Brealey Publishing
Boston • London

First published by Davies-Black, an imprint of Nicholas Brealey Publishing, in 2009.

20 Park Plaza, Suite 1115A
Boston, MA 02116, USA
Tel: + 617-523-3801
Fax: + 617-523-3708

3–5 Spafield Street, Clerkenwell
London, EC1R 4QB, UK
Tel: +44-(0)-207-239-0360
Fax: +44-(0)-207-239-0370

www.nicholasbrealey.com

Special discounts on bulk quantities of Davies-Black books are available to corporations, professional associations, and other organizations. For details, contact us at 888-273-2539.

Printed in the United States of America.

13 12 11 10 09 10 9 8 7 6 5 4 3 2 1

ISBN: 978-0-89106-284-4

Library of Congress Cataloging-in-Publication Data

Kaputa, Catherine, 1948–
    The female brand : using the female mindset to succeed in business/ Catherine Kaputa.
        p. cm.
    Includes bibliographical references and index.
    ISBN 978-0-89106-284-4 (hardcover)
    1. Businesswomen.   2. Success in business.   I. Title.
    HD6053.K37 2009
    658.4'09082—dc22   2008048675

For my mother,

Carmen Lockwood Kaputa,

and all the mothers like her,
who have inspired countless millions
since the dawn of time

CONTENTS

PREFACE

New World—New Woman

Ever since a certain assertive female decided she wanted to eat fruit from a certain forbidden tree, women have been loved, hated, glorified, vilified, and misunderstood. Our modern world, of course, is no different. Today, however, in many ways we are shedding the rigid ideas that were commonplace just a generation ago and venturing into a brave new world of adventure, opportunity, and angst.

Women first entered the workplace in great numbers out of necessity in World War II. The enormity of the war effort meant that millions of men would need to be mobilized for the task. Men couldn't be in two places at once. So if men were busy driving jeeps, who was making the jeeps?

Rosie the Riveter, that's who.

Quaint notions of the weaker sex and a woman's place were swept aside in an instant. Saving the world came first. Victory brought the men back to the factories, but nothing could bring back the world that had been. Changes to come would, for better or worse, remake the family, the workplace, and the world.

To understand the future of the workplace, it's important to realize how relatively new our economic reality is. Well into the twentieth century, women's lives were centered around home and family, as were most men's, since most people still lived on the farm. The so-called industrial revolution laid the foundation of our current commercial world. Commerce, of course, has always existed, but it has become an overwhelming presence and has dramatically affected our lives.

In a blink of historical time, we've gone from making our own clothes and growing our own food to making only money. Stereotypes of women have changed dramatically in my lifetime alone. When I was growing up in the 1950s and '60s, women were viewed as not-quite-as-good versions of men. Women of my generation were encouraged to go after "pink" jobs like nursing and teaching. While these are worthwhile pursuits, why should women be limited?

In the '70s, the women's liberation movement threw a torch at thinking pink and claimed that there are no differences between men and women, only stereotypes. We could be and do anything. Women started going after all kinds of jobs and succeeding. Storming the gates of the male workplace, though, came at a cost for women. We had to submerge our families and try to be superwomen.

Science created another sea change that affected the role of women in society. Women's biological role was revolutionized, and women were liberated in attitude, biology, and opportunity.

But opportunity means the *chance* to succeed. It doesn't mean things are equal or that you *will* succeed. If only it were that simple! Things are not necessarily equal for men, either, though it's women who typically have to go the extra mile. Nevertheless, a major change is taking place today, too, as companies embrace diversity in the workforce.

Today, women are influencing the workplace, and many companies are trying to make it easier for women, with diversity or women's initiatives, flextime, and opt-out programs that accommodate child rearing. Even though the image of women in the workplace has evolved dramatically, we're still not where we want to be. We're still in transition.

The number of women in the workforce continues to increase, mainly because women do a good job—particularly with our modern jobs. As the Western world moves further and further away from basic manufacturing work and as machines replace people, cooperation, verbal skills, organization, and teamwork are more valued. Increasingly, skills and temperaments considered more female than male are what help make one successful in the twenty-first century.

Remarkable new research on gender differences in neuroscience, psychology, and social science questions the original women's liberation notion that men and women are the same. In many ways, the most revealing research, and the hardest to deny, comes from the emerging field of neuroscience because it uses magnetic resonance imaging (MRI) and positron-emission tomography (PET) scans to record what actually takes place in the brains of women and men as they perform different activities. There is also a lively debate about gender issues taking place among evolutionary psychologists, who look at evolution as the basis for the development of gender differences and culture.

Many gender differences show up in studies of behavior dynamics. One landmark study involved male and female children—prepubescent children, so that even the influence of hormones is eliminated as much as possible.[1] The study demonstrates some basic differences in approach that are germane to the workplace and society in general. These differences are reflected in what I call a "male brand" and a "female brand." Children were separated into all-boy and all-girl groups and given a task to complete cooperatively. The girls used their social skills and worked together and formed a kind of committee. They all took part in discussions about how to accomplish the task. Meanwhile, the boys jostled around and picked a leader, and then the leader directed the effort to get the job done.

Both in their way had positive outcomes. But each gender used very different models. When the groups were given tasks that were too hard or difficult to accomplish, the boys wound up screaming and fighting among themselves, while the girls became moody and withdrawn.

Yes, there are downsides to gender, too. When things are out of whack, men are more likely to sink into antisocial behaviors like violence, aggression, and alcohol abuse, while women tend to turn inward and experience eating disorders, panic attacks, and depression.[2]

I became intrigued with the larger question: Is there a female brand distinct from the male variety? And what are its advantages in the workplace? Is our biology, in fact, not a weakness that we should try to ignore while hoping for it to disappear?

Of course, in many areas, there aren't significant differences between women and men. But I have become convinced that in other ways there are important differences in aptitude, preference, and motivation that have a big effect on women's approach to their professional and personal lives. Just as we each have individual strengths based on who we are as people, we have gender-based strengths as women that are important assets of the female brand.

The female mindset has incredible aptitudes. We form deep friendships and foster peaceful interpersonal relations. We're great at forming teams and working cooperatively to get a complex task done. We're big-picture thinkers and planners. Women have a heightened ability to read people and see emotion, even in extremely subtle demonstrations. Our heightened intuitive and empathetic skills can be a distinct advantage in our cooperative social workplace.

Now, the disclaimer. Female qualities are not limited to women. We all have both male and female in us. And it's possible for a man to be more female than a woman. As groups, men are more masculine and women are more feminine, but as individuals, that's not necessarily so.

(Just as, in general, men are taller than women, but plenty of women are taller than plenty of men—just ask Katie Holmes or Tom Cruise.) The point is that men can learn from getting in touch with their feminine side as much as women can.

In my personal branding talks, coaching, and interviews with women, I started exploring how successful women take advantage of their female mindset and assets along with their personal strengths and skills. A core idea of personal branding is that the better you understand yourself, both strengths and weaknesses, the easier it will be to maximize your strong points and compensate for the weak points.

As I thought about *The Female Brand*, I considered my twenty-plus years working in a wide variety of organizations and all the challenges and people I've met along the way. I certainly did my fair share of moving around, from the cultural world of art museums to the advertising world of Madison Avenue, from marketing financial products on Wall Street to teaching branding in the halls of academe. I've experienced the entrepreneurial highs and lows of running my own personal-brand strategy business. And I began reminiscing about the experiences and the people, particularly the successful women I'd met along the way.

In one of my flashbacks, I was transported back to my first days at the ad agency Wells, Rich, Greene, with its female CEO, Mary Wells Lawrence. The offices at Wells, Rich, Greene were not like the rest of Madison Avenue, just as a sturdy oxford is not like a dainty pump. It was feminine. As soon as you entered the lobby, you felt the warmth and richness of an elegant Park Avenue manse, with vibrant wall treatments, carefully chosen colors and textures, tasteful art and antiques. This was not your typical corporate office.

A grand staircase was the focal point of the agency. It would be easy to imagine Vivien Leigh or Loretta Young sweeping down elegantly with her skirt gently swaying as she descended. The staircase, naturally, led to Mary's suite of offices. We would meet with clients in the Jade Room or the Duck Room, which I usually chose because its collection of antique duck decoys showed that femininity is complex and not limited to frills, lace, and the color pink.

All the ad execs' offices were fitted out with antique or sleek modern furniture, and what you chose mattered to Mary. A very senior female executive made the mistake of selecting without the proper gravity. When Mary came by and saw her simple Parsons table and bare walls, the next visitor was a moving crew replacing the entire contents of the room. Afterward, this executive had a darling French provincial desk, striking paisley drapes, and trendy Andy Warhol sketches of flowers on the wall.

Mary Wells Lawrence's unabashedly feminine style as a leader permeated the agency, from the stylish look of the offices, to the personal leadership style she fostered and the way client relationships were nurtured, to the panache of the creative work and our drive to go the extra mile and do our best.

The female mindset was part of her edge.

INTRODUCTION

Gender can be a sensitive issue. Some women, because of past stereotyping, may be skittish about even just exploring gender differences. They don't want to be pegged again with "biology is destiny" or turn back feminism's accomplishments. And who can blame them? My goal is certainly not to continue unfair stereotypes but to provide new insights into the uniqueness of the female mindset and how women can maximize career and life success by using *all* their assets. That means building on your personal strengths, intelligence, and talent, but it also means leveraging your native strengths, instincts, and preferences as a woman: empathy, verbal agility, people orientation, a collaborative leadership style, and visual identity, among other assets. It means thinking in a new way, because the standard brand in business is the male brand. In short, it means thinking and acting to develop your own female brand.

Using all of your assets also means understanding the perceptions in the workplace about women (and yourself individually) so that you can override them or know how far you can push things. After all, none of us works in a vacuum. We work with men and women who often have strong perceptions (right or wrong) about the female brand that are different from perceptions about the male brand. To deny that these perceptions exist is to invite failure. To understand these perceptions gives us power, for then we can disarm them or use them to our advantage.

For many of us, the problem is that we don't realize we have an edge. We don't know how to create positive perceptions about ourselves in the workplace. We have trouble building a personal brand or finding the right career and a fulfilling life. Many of us are insecure about our power, particularly if we work in a male-dominated company (and most of us do). But the reality is that we have more power than we think we have.

This book will show you how to find your power and use it. Each chapter focuses on the aptitudes of the female mindset and on the essential building blocks for branding yourself for success with practical advice and examples. Each chapter begins with a quote from a successful professional woman and ends with a female-brand profile, a real-life, first-person account of the personal career journey of an amazing

woman and her thoughts on success. Interspersed throughout are stories and advice from other career women—of different ages, in different professions, with different experiences—minus identifying details
and last names in order to protect their privacy. Each chapter contains
Brainstormer exercises that you can do yourself, applying the chapter's
ideas to your own career. After all, you don't want to just read about
theories and the success of others; you want to create your own edge.

Thinking like a brand is integral to my approach to career success;
it reflects my background in branding and advertising and my work in
personal branding. Applying principles and tactics from the commercial world of brands is a smart way to create more success in your life.
Branding enables you to think of yourself as a "product" in a competitive marketplace and to differentiate yourself from competitors. It
enables you to think outside-in, that is, thinking first of what the market wants and then strategically positioning yourself to meet those needs.
Branding forces you to think strategically and creatively as you build an
authentic and powerful visual and verbal identity. And no brand would
be effective without up-to-date tactics for forging ahead in tough circumstances.

One of our great reservoirs of wisdom is made up of memorable
quotes—small sayings that have endured with countless repetitions
because they tell us something about the human experience and about
ourselves. I wanted inspiring quotes for this book, and, as I got into the
project, all of a sudden I realized I knew a woman whose words were
more influential to me, in a way, than even Shakespeare's. Mom. My
mother is priceless. And many of the women I interviewed also cited
their mothers as the person they most admire. So this book is peppered
throughout with quotable wisdom from that other great Bard, my mom.

I've often said to my brother and sisters that if our mother had been
born later, she would be a CEO running a global company; that's how
good she was at running things. She stayed home when we were young,
sewed all our clothes, cleaned the house, cooked our meals, and made
sure we all did our homework and got good grades. She was the CEO
of the family.

I wouldn't be the woman I am today without her as my mom. Mom
always told me that I could be anyone I wanted to be and do anything
I wanted to do, and that was at a time when girls were encouraged to

become teachers if they were smart. She framed my artwork, but the best thing she framed was me.

Of course, there is no silver bullet that guarantees you'll reach your dreams, not even having a wise mom as a mentor. If only there were. We'd all love to know the precise series of steps to take—the hurdles we need to jump, the exact list of items we need to check off—that will guarantee our success. There are many things we can do to enhance our chances of success, but, except for two famous things we would all rather avoid, there are no sure things in life.

But some things are clearly necessary if you want to be a successful woman today. No matter whether you are an executive, a professional, an entrepreneur, a consultant, a coach, an artist, a boomer running a nonprofit in your retirement, or a mom with a Web site and something to sell, you must craft an identity that's true to you and right for the marketplace—a distinct personal brand—and you must create positive perceptions about yourself in the marketplace.

The Female Brand is a how-to and how-to-think book for women of all ages who want to create more success, fulfillment, or options. We're all familiar with the numbers: Women make up 51 percent of the workforce, yet even today, in 2008, more than forty years after the feminist revolution rocked the country, only a paltry 2 percent of Fortune 500 CEOs are women.[1]

The Female Brand will provide new insights into why it's different for women in the workplace, how to tap into the aptitudes we're wired for as women, and why playing our game the way men play their game usually backfires. We need to lead with our XX chromosomes!

This book is a high-octane guide for women who want to avoid getting stuck and who want to build a powerful self-brand, network, and confidence—a guide to thriving in today's male-dominated but soon-to-be-female-dominated workplace.

After all, men don't leave their gender-based advantages at the door when they go to work. Neither should women.

The biggest factors in my success were knowing my stuff and doing a good job, as well as being strong and independent. I refused to be intimidated by difficult men. I cultivated a tough, can-do attitude and insisted on making it on merit without any special favors. Once, at a company baseball game, I even walked off in a huff when they tried to bend the rules for me and give me more than three strikes. I just wanted a level playing field where performance counts. I don't do female engineering. I do engineering.

Barbara Res
engineer on Trump Tower

I

TRUE TO NATURE

Do you know this woman? She could be your college roommate. She could be working in your office. Or she could be living in your body. She's someone who feels she needs to make a change. She doesn't lack talent or a work ethic, but her life and career don't seem to be on the right track. And she's afraid the train might derail completely. Or maybe she'll just get off the train and walk home.

She knows her workplace has modern attitudes. Her boss may even be a woman. But something is still wrong. She's unsure of herself. She's not living up to her potential. She's frustrated. She's good at multitasking, but the push-pull of work and family can be just too much.

She's suffering from a problem that affects only women: female behavior confusion disorder.

Too Hot? Too Cold?

What's a woman to do? How do you get it right in the workplace?

Your instincts may tell you to "be nice," but be too nice and you might not be taken seriously. If you are too assertive and exhibit the same leadership qualities that are praised in a man, you risk that familiar epithet referring to a female dog that, curiously, has no male equivalent.

Even Catalyst, the research organization that's been studying the "female brand" and the workforce for thirty years, isn't sure. But at least it knows we're in a double bind. Its 2007 study "Damned If You Do, Doomed If You Don't" found that women face three double-bind dilemmas:[1]

- **Can't-win perceptions.** If women act like women, they are perceived as weak. If they act like men, they are viewed as too tough.
- **Higher bar—low reward.** Women have to work harder and often receive less.
- **Competent yet disliked.** Women with successful male leadership skills such as assertiveness are often disliked.

It's the Goldilocks dilemma. If you're too hot, you're branded as out of control. If you're too cold, you're labeled an ice queen. The same behavior that's acceptable in a man is often criticized in a woman. It's almost impossible to get it just right.

How Do You Cope?

It's a woman's dilemma. Whether we supported her or not, many of us felt Hillary Clinton's pain when she ran for president of the United States in 2008.[2] Or we cringed in sympathy or embarrassment for Sarah Palin when she ran for vice president that same year. Both women had to struggle with female behavior confusion disorder, too.

We could identify with the challenges Clinton and Palin faced as female candidates trying to get into the boys club. Many of us have faced similar difficulties in the professional world, especially if we're ambitious and interested in doing more, or if we've tried to break new ground in a role that was previously male-only turf. From a marketing perspective, we're female brands trying to get shelf space in a market dominated and controlled by male brands.

It's one thing for Clinton and Palin to be critiqued on their politics and point of views, but their hair and clothing were also critiqued. Nothing was off limits, not even Sarah's shoes or the thickness of Hillary's ankles. In debates with male opponents, each woman's voice, pitch, and tone were scrutinized, not just the content of their answers.

Laughing too loud or coming close to tears in front of a reporter was a big media story for Hillary—even her authenticity was called into question after she choked up when asked how she copes each day. And then to top it all off, there was CBS reporter Katie Couric's interview of Sarah Palin that was famously channeled by Tina Fey on *Saturday Night Live*. In one swoop, Palin got branded as a ditz, Couric's hard-news credentials were refurbished, and Fey's star power shot into the stratosphere.

You're Not a Man

The conventional wisdom has been that women have trouble succeeding because they don't act like men, the top-selling brand in the career marketplace. The advice we've been given is to try to act like a man in the workplace. So we took courses and tried to be more assertive. In the past, we were even encouraged to "dress for success," which meant like a man, so we turned to dark, skirted suits with shoulder pads, briefcases, and tie-like scarves. Or we tried to adopt the male command-and-control model. Or we tried to model ourselves after male leaders in our company.

If that's the conventional wisdom, it's wrong. Playing it like a man doesn't work. Acting like a man brands you as tough and aggressive. When women adopt attitudes such as forcefulness and assertiveness, we are lambasted as "too tough" and "unfeminine."

I remember a certain female executive back when I first worked on Wall Street. We'll call her "Alex." She was smart and got the job done, and done well. But her ideas on team building and compassion came right out of Joseph Stalin's playbook. Alex played the tough guy so well, you could imagine her as a fire-eater in the circus. Alex behaved like a bully and everyone was afraid of her, even her own staff. Alex represented what I hoped was a dying breed, a type not much discussed in women's leadership circles—the tough, successful female who is mean to other women and tries to sabotage them.

One day she called me to complain about a member of my staff, "Sophia," who had the audacity to disagree with the recommendation one of Alex's people had made in a meeting. And Alex complained to me about it in typical Alex fashion. "Tell your person if she does it again, I'll break her [expletive deleted] kneecaps."

Ouch! I didn't pass along Alex's stupid threat but counseled Sophia to always use all the diplomatic skills she could muster when talking with Alex or anyone on Alex's staff.

> *Bad behavior is disliked in a man.*
> *But it's despised in a woman.*

This sort of behavior is counterproductive and ultimately destructive. A few years later, as usually happens, Alex had a big project that blew up. She needed some supporters to rally around her and maybe put the blowup in perspective. Unfortunately for her, but fortunately for the company and everyone else, Alex had no supporters and left the firm. The reign of terror was over, and we all gave a big sigh of relief. Her bad reputation was so well known in the industry that she was never able to land a big job again.

Be Who You Are—A Woman

Trying to act like a man is stupid for the most basic reason. We're not men! And that's an advantage!

It's common sense to be authentic, and it's smart branding. Great commercial brands are always built on authenticity and on a brand's inherent strengths, and it's the same with you. Your brand must come from who you are, what makes you tick, what your passions are, and what your strengths are, even what your biology dictates. Confidence comes from being comfortable in your own skin.

You'll avoid the stress of trying to be something you're not and constantly attempting to fix your shortcomings. You'll be worth more as well.

The choice is between increasing results using your aptitudes and assets or making minor improvements to weak areas that will probably never be a major strength. Your house of cards may eventually collapse around you. Don't shortchange your assets and your power.

Tune In to Your Wiring

Turns out Mom was right. She always said, "Boys will be boys and girls will be girls."

We *are* wired differently. "Not that there's anything wrong with that," to quote Jerry Seinfeld. We don't need a million-dollar research study to tell us that what we are and how we are—how we think and how we behave—are different. Just go to a playground and watch girls and boys play.

I used to think that many gender differences resulted from being raised differently. To say that our biology has some effect on our minds and how we see the world still strikes some as un-American. We shouldn't be determined by anything, right? But once I had a son, I could see with my own eyes how differently the genders are wired from the beginning. How much is due to genes? How much to hormones? Trying to eliminate any taint from the social environment, Professor Simon Baron-Cohen videotaped more than one hundred infants at one day old. His study showed that baby girls were most attracted to a mobile of a face, and baby boys were more fixated on a mechanical mobile.[3]

It's fascinating to watch the toys that each gender likes to play with. By and large, girls are more fascinated with faces and people—by dolls and playing house. Boys are fascinated by things—by cars and construction sets. Both casual observation and academic studies by Baron-Cohen and others confirm these preferences.

So how does this play out in life—girls and people versus boys and things?

One basic difference is women's tendency to be more social and to focus on people and connection. We tend to have good radar for detecting the effect we have on others and sensing their feelings. And that can be a two-edged sword. One study focused on fourth-grade Israeli children running on a track. There was no speed difference between the boys and girls until competition was thrown into the mix. When they were put in paired groups to run, the boys ran faster and the girls ran slower. And the girls ran slowest of all when running with another girl.[4]

In contrast to a woman's interest in empathy and connection, studies by Baron-Cohen and others show that men have a more outward orientation and focus on understanding and building systems. Of course there are exceptions, but on the whole women are a people-oriented brand and men are a thing-oriented brand.

The female brain is hardwired for empathy and connection.
The male brain is hardwired for building systems.

Hormones rev up our natural instincts toward connection even more. As girls become teens, they focus even more on personal emotions and intimate relationships, because when estrogen floods the brain, it bolsters female social skills with an intense drive toward connection.[4] Estrogen and oxytocin also help power women's intuition and empathy. Motherhood brings about more changes and hormones, driving an overriding urge to nurture, avoid conflict, and build connection with others. With menopause, women experience a final shift in hormones. Estrogen and oxytocin are lower. Now, rather than being driven by a desire to connect with and nurture others, we women, often for the first time, focus on ourselves. At last we give ourselves permission to do our own thing.

The Female Brain

Because some gender studies have displayed contradictory results, one of the hottest areas in gender research is the field of neuroscience, which studies the structure and function of the brain and nervous system. While the male and female brains are similar in so many ways, neuroscientific studies point to some female advantages and aptitudes: strong empathetic ability, verbal skills, keen emotional responsiveness, and other advantages

To make their discoveries, neuroscientists use a four-ton device called a functional magnetic resonance imaging (fMRI) scanner. These machines record changes in the oxygen level of blood feeding the brain. Because the brain rapidly supplies blood to working areas, active areas virtually light up to provide a mini-movie of what's going on. A "brain-to-brain dance" takes place when we connect with another person, and different areas of the brain "light up" during certain activities in men and in women.

One interesting difference shown in the MRI pictures is that most women use both the right and left hemispheres of the brain for processing verbal, visual, and emotional experiences. Men use only one.[6] The bundle of nerves connecting the two hemispheres is also thicker in women, making for a wide boulevard of connection. And that's not the end of it. A neuroscientist counted the neurons in the brain tissue of men and women—thin slice by thin slice—and found that the female brain is densely packed with 11 percent more neurons in the language area.[7]

Most women are smaller than men, and the female brain is about 9 percent smaller. This size advantage led some scientists to speculate that men were smarter than women.[8] But it turns out that women have just as many brain cells as men. Our brain cells are just packed more tightly into a smaller braincase.

Intelligence

Women are just as intelligent as men, too, if you look at average IQ scores. But men tend to overestimate their brainpower, and women underestimate their smarts, what one researcher dubbed the "male hubris, female humility effect."[9] This tendency to play dumb about our intellectual capabilities is something we must resist. People might believe us!

> *The average IQ of women and men is about even,*
> *though men tend to* overestimate *and*
> *women tend to* underestimate *their intelligence.*

Memories of old-fashioned thinking about female intellectual ability added fuel to the fire that engulfed Lawrence Summers, the former president of Harvard University. In 2005, Summers made a remark in a speech questioning whether the relative scarcity of women in science was due to innate differences in ability between men and women. The story took on a life of its own in the media, and Summers's comments generated such a storm of protest that he thought it best to resign.

It's true that there are fewer women working in the sciences and math, but it's not lack of ability that is holding us back. Tests show that women can do math and science extremely well.[10]

Perhaps science and math aren't presented in the right way for women, and these fields have a male brand-image (the computer nerd) that discourages women, similar to the guys-only image of top corporate jobs.

The real reason may be the simplest and most profound. Many women aren't interested in math and science as careers. Women often think of math and science as too abstract and systems oriented (a male preference) and not sufficiently people and content oriented (a female preference). One study showed that people who liked to work with tools or machines were more likely to choose information technology careers. People who liked working with people were a lot less likely to choose IT careers (more women fall into this camp).[11]

Preferences and Options

One landmark study followed more than three thousand mathematically precocious boys and girls from middle school to middle age over a thirty-five-year period. All were gifted in math, but when it came time to choose a career, a chasm emerged.[12] The men selected engineering and physical sciences, and the women were more likely to choose medicine, biological sciences, humanities, and the social sciences.

In short, this large-scale study over three decades showed that mathematically strong men prefer to work with "inorganic" things in fields involving machines, abstractions, and the like. The women, in general, prefer to work with "organic" or living things in fields involving social interaction with people and helping people.

Something else in this study was startling. The women had more options. Women who were gifted in math were more likely than the men to have strong verbal skills, too. So they could choose careers in science or become lawyers, marketers, or teachers. The males who were good in math tended to have weak verbal skills.

This gender divide in the sciences is greatest in countries that allow women the most freedom to choose. For example, there are five to seven times more females in the hard sciences (such as physics) in Russia and the Philippines than in Canada, the United Kingdom, or the United States. And most of the girls who succeed in math in the U.S. are immigrants or the daughters of immigrants.[13]

As barriers come down, gender gaps seem to widen. With more opportunities, we have choices. For most women, a career in technology or the hard sciences doesn't match our DNA. We're in a culture where math and IT have a decidedly male, nerdy brand image. It doesn't fit our brand unless it's a people-oriented job like medicine or a people-oriented role like sales and marketing in a technology or science company. And it's doable. About 70 percent of the jobs in IT companies are nonprogramming jobs and are highly "organic," involving strong interpersonal skills.[14]

If, like many women, we're good at both, we may like math but love literature and the humanities. This is freedom.

Take the Middle Road

Gender expert Roy Baumeister points out that men go to extremes more than women do. He says that we can see this male-female dichotomy in intelligence, in height, in on-the-job risk taking, in status, and in society.[15]

Look at intelligence, which, as we pointed out, is about equal. Men are more often at the extremes here, too. There are more men at the top of the IQ heap and also more men at the bottom. There are fewer women at the extremes and more in the middle range in intelligence. But overall, average intelligence is about equal.

Look at the business, social, or political pecking order. Men are running most things—at the very top, running large companies and leading nations—but there are more men at the other extreme, too. There are more men by far at the very bottom of society, locked up in our prisons. (Women made up 7 percent of the prison population in 2006.)[16]

Men typically are viewed as the stronger sex, but they are also the weaker sex. Fewer boys than girls survive through birth. Men are more likely by far to have developmental and learning disorders like attention deficit disorder. As adults, men on average have more illnesses and die younger than women (an average life span of seventy-eight years for men versus eighty-four years for women).[17]

Tap into the Female Leadership Style

Of course, each of us develops her own personal leadership style, but there are characteristics of the female brand that many of us instinctually gravitate toward. We tend to have a big-picture orientation. Women leaders are more like mentors or coaches, favoring collaboration, involving colleagues in making decisions, and nurturing the various members of the team. We tend to be highly intuitive and more people oriented in making leadership decisions and more service oriented in dealing with clients.[18] We can be great talent developers, and at the end of the day, the quality of the people can make the difference between a company that does just OK and one that clicks.

Again, it's a generalization, but the male brand tends to be more of a command-and-control type. Men are often more objective and analytical in making leadership decisions. The male style is powerful, too, with its focus on analysis and getting the system to work in the best way.

What you want to do is to lead with a style that's natural to you, and don't try to be like a man if that's not your style. Otherwise, we won't use what's different and powerful about our exceptional advantages and style, our singular abilities and sensibilities, which can give the female brand an edge in the workplace and everyplace.

Leverage Your Female Edge

Branding is about leveraging your edge over competitive brands. The female mindset gives us powerful aptitudes that we should leverage in the workplace for career success:

- **Exceptional empathy.** We've got antennae that are terrific at reading gestures, tone of voice, faces, and postures. In short, we can read between the lines and know what's really going on with someone.
- **Uncanny intuition.** We can go with our gut. We often know the answer through an unconscious process that can be remarkably accurate and insightful.
- **Strong verbal and communication skills.** Women score better in reading comprehension, writing, and other verbal skills, all of which are crucial in the workplace.
- **The social gene and the ability to build deep personal relationships.** Women are better at connecting with and nurturing other people. Women specialize in building strong, supportive relationships.
- **More openness in communicating and sharing feelings.** Women are more willing to open up, start talking, and share their emotions. We are more likely to speak out about problems that are affecting morale in the workplace.
- **Collaborative, team-oriented leadership style.** Rather than turning to a command-and-control leadership style, women tend to build consensus and lead with active group participation.
- **More appearance tools at our disposal.** Women can use their flair and sense of style to create a stronger visual identity through

clothing, hairstyles, makeup, and accessories—a core component of personal branding.

Try the Brainstormer below to explore your female attributes.

BRAINSTORMER

Leverage Your Female Edge

How do you stack up in the *female strengths* most women are biologically wired for? Write down your thoughts about your aptitudes:

Empathy: your ability to connect with others through a sense of similarity

Intuition: your ability to sense what's really going on in a situation

Verbal ability: your overall communication skills in writing and speaking

People skills: your social gene and ability to connect with others

Leadership: your personal leadership style

Visual identity: your self-presentation

Work the Female-Brand Advantage

Look at the aptitudes of males and females listed below. Of course, none is carved in stone for any individual, but they represent tendencies and orientations wired into most of us because of our gender. As women, we have strong proficiencies based on our verbal prowess, our keen abilities to read the room and connect with people, and our collaborative and community-building skills. These characteristics are essential to brand building. Even our variety and range of personal style and wardrobe give us an advantage in building a strong visual identity. It's a brand manager's dream.

MALE MINDSET	FEMALE MINDSET
Commander	Team leader
Individuality	Connection
Competition	Collaboration
Narrower focus	Big picture
Facts and figures	Story and context
Reason	Intuition
Employees	Community
Analysis	Empathy
More and shallower relationships	Fewer and deeper relationships
Large groups	Small groups
More homogenous appearance	More differentiated appearance
Thinker	Feeler
Things and systems	People
Spatial ability	Language ability

Nurture What You Want to Grow

So many things shape us—our family and friends, the education we receive, and the times we grow up, in along with our biology, our evolutionary history, and our genes.

The interesting thing is that what we nurture is what grows in us. And neuroscientists are proving it. Scientists talk of "neuroplasticity"— how what we experience and focus on can actually "sculpt" the shape, size, and number of neurons, even the thickness of the connections between them.[19] It's like Mom always said: "Use it or lose it."

Many of us begin with great callings and then move on to duties and demands. But often we're great at managing priorities—at least, everyone's priorities but our own.

We need to put ourselves and our career success back into the equation. We need to leverage our personal strengths and our aptitudes as women. It's not helpful to blame the old boy network or the glass ceiling. We need to focus on what we can control and on our best assets— our personal strengths and the aptitudes we're wired for as women.

The goal is to be ourselves, have fun and succeed, and maybe even make the world a little better place.

We're women, after all.

DREAMS ARE FOR LIVING

Meenu Chhabra
president and CEO, biotechnology company

My childhood was full of mixed messages about the role of women in society. My mother, like my father, had a PhD, but she lived the life of a traditional Indian woman. Mother always told me, "You are equal to any man," but she knew that she was not a role model for gender equality.

My background made me determined to lead by example as well as words in my life. I strive for bold and clear communication in my career and urge women to speak in a large voice and never be intimidated by male bravado.

My mother's acquiescence to the status quo when she had so much potential caused me to strive aggressively for high achievement. I was twenty-two by the time I finally rebelled against my father's backward ideas and had my first date. I trained as a neuropsychopharmacologist and earned an MBA.

My goals in life were fueled by desires to travel and to create things that hadn't existed before. I first worked in Italy but then moved to a Swiss multinational pharmaceutical company, which allowed me to travel the world and learn about deal making and cultural differences.

I was often the youngest person as well as the only female in meetings. This helped strengthen my brand as being exceptional. Being young and female can help open doors, but then you need to prove your ability to stay there. I knew I was destined to run a company like I'm doing now. Working in the biotech field on vital, breakthrough endeavors like curing disease is a dream come true. It's always challenging to be a CEO, but being young and a woman compounds those challenges. My strategy is to find brilliant people and let them know that I depend on them to teach me things. I'm not an isolated figurehead, and I can be wrong. I want them to feel that they can say anything to me.

Women's lives are often more complex than men's. Women have more to juggle besides their careers. They generally have the primary role to play with the children and the myriad things that take place in a family's life. So women have to think in terms of what's important to them and then simplify their lives around that. When I mentor ambitious women, here's what I say:

- **Determine your priorities.** If your first priority is your children, focus on situations that will give you maximum quality time with your family.
- **Create a career goal.** If your goal is to become a CEO, determine when you would like to achieve that and build a plan backward from there.
- **Get a career coach.** Objective advice from someone without an agenda is crucial.
- **Identify personal champions.** It is vital to create personal champions who are senior, well connected, and respected—

people who can alert you to leads before anyone else knows about them.

- **Treat your job search like a business deal.** Know the terms you would like and identify partners willing to give you those terms.

"You are equal to any man" is no longer an abstract notion for women. There are gender issues, of course, but more and more those differences are recognized as strengths.

I've learned there are no limits. I have a lot more I want to accomplish as CEO, but I also want to sail around the world, grow olives in Spain, create great photographs, raise a beautiful child, and be an inspiring example.

I was originally planning to go to law school, but it hit me that as a lawyer, I'd always be saying no to other people. I wanted to find a job opportunity where the answers would be not no but yes!

Marcia Roosevelt
executive vice president,
Saatchi & Saatchi

2

BRANDING FOR SUCCESS

A branding maven once said, "There is no 'and' in 'brand.'" Of course, the letters are there, but the advice means that you shouldn't define yourself as an accountant and an actress and an interior designer, as someone once described herself to me at a networking event.

Being a "this and that" person may be interesting on the cocktail party circuit, but it's a temptation you must be careful to avoid. You'll be much more successful with your career identity if you let go of extraneous portions of your identity to focus on a singular brand. Otherwise, people won't know what to make of you. You risk being branded "Jill of All Trades, Master of None." That's why it pays to be familiar with the basics of Branding 101.

Self-branding means being able to articulate a simple, clear expression of who you are, doing it consistently, and delivering on it again and again, so that when people think of X, they think of you. Or when people think of you, they think of X.

Some women, concerned with authenticity, think branding is fake. But good branding is always built on authenticity, although it's a simplified you that emphasizes what's most valuable about your many aptitudes. All the complexity of who you are is too confusing.

When you start thinking of yourself as a brand, you discover how powerful it can be. Rather than being viewed generically as one of the worker bees, you'll be someone who stands for something distinct and desirable—a brand.

❋　　❋　　❋

A self-brand is an identity that
sticks like peanut butter in the minds of others.

❋　　❋　　❋

In today's overcommunicated society, the brands that stand for something relevant and build positive perceptions are the ones that succeed. It's the same with people. In today's overcompetitive society, people who build a career identity—a personal brand—that has relevance and visibility in the marketplace will have the advantage.

That's why marketers figure out the big idea they can best use to leverage a brand, drum away at it consistently, and evolve it slowly over time.

Keep Your Brand Focused

Complexity gets in the way of smart branding. Brands that try to be too many things generally don't do well because we don't know what to make of them. When we meet a Jill of All Trades, we always wonder how good she is at any one thing if she is doing so many completely different things. Plus she's perceived as having a weak commitment to the main thing. So don't think that focusing your brand or targeting a specific market niche is limiting and restricts opportunity. You'll find that the opposite is true. The more specifically you define who you are, the better your chance of selling yourself.

How you define and brand yourself is something you should think about. Like it or not, we organize and understand the world by putting things into different slots or pigeonholes. This brand is good for this. That brand is good for that. That's the way people think.

The branding principle of singularity doesn't mean you can't have a fairly wide brand footprint, either. But if you are defining yourself with a slash identity, it's best to have a perceptual linkage, so that the ideas complement each other. You can be a businessperson/philanthropist, an accountant/female activist, a consultant/speaker/writer, or a stockbroker/financial literacy activist. Or you can meld your diverse talents into something new. For instance, my colleague Carol, an engineer who loved helping her friends, became a leadership coach who leverages technology to help clients increase their visibility.

The branding principle of singularity also doesn't mean you can't change your brand and career identity into something completely different, either. Products do, and you can, too, with careful branding.

Vive la Différence

The cardinal rule of branding is to be different. Being just like everyone else will stunt your success. You'll be anonymous—like a mass-produced person who's indistinguishable from others on the assembly line. People will define you in terms of others, and as a clone, you'll always be a B player.

Some people begin developing a self-brand by modeling themselves after successful people they admire, often people in their company. This has always been somewhat of a dilemma for women because there aren't a lot of female role models.

But even if you do look to others for ideas on how to model your brand, you always have to take it a step further. You have to refashion your brand based on what's authentic and different about you. You need to be yourself but stretch. You have to struggle against conformity if you want to find your own identity. After all, as Walt Whitman told us, "What you are, picks its way."

You need to figure out your own big idea—what's different, relevant, and special about you—so that you can compete in today's flat world. To do that, begin the traditional branding process with a brand audit, an analysis of the brand and key competitors. Part of the brand audit is the SWOT (strengths, weaknesses, opportunities, threats) analysis listed in the Brainstormer on page 20.

Another approach marketers use is to think in terms of metaphor or analogy. What's different about a product (or you) may be difficult to explain and requires time for people to digest. But if you use a metaphor, anchoring the brand in something people already know, you short-circuit the process and enhance the brand's appeal. The key is to "anchor and twist"—anchor the idea in something familiar but give it your own twist, like Apple did with the iPhone.[1] You don't want to be an imitator; you want to be like "*X* on steroids," or "a cross between *X* and *Y*," or "like *A* meets *B*."

You can also link different strengths to create your big idea. Look at Scott Adams, the creator of *Dilbert*. It's hard to be truly brilliant at one thing, but almost everybody, Adams feels, can be in the top 25 percent of two or even three things.[2] And that's what he did in forming his own brand. Adams strung together drawing (he was a good but not a great artist), business savvy (not great at office politics but a good

BRAINSTORMER

SWOT Analysis

You can do this yourself or ask colleagues and friends for their input:

Strengths. Write down anything that you are good at and love to do, or what your boss or clients give you high marks on. Look at the list of female aptitudes in chapter I. Which do you feel are strengths in yourself?

Weaknesses. Write down what you're terrible at and hate to do, or what your boss and friends criticize you for.

Opportunities. This is wide open. Write down anything that could be an opportunity for you. A key is to look for unmet or unsatisfied needs that you could capitalize on.

Threats. Write down what keeps you awake at night, whether real or imagined, about yourself, your career, or your business.

observer), and humor. He was in the top 25 percent in these attributes, but when he put them together, he created a powerful unique selling proposition—and created *Dilbert*.

You can also look into in-person assessments or online tests like the *Strong Interest Inventory*® instrument. Assessments and personality inventories can be a great starting point on your personal brand journey. But don't expect an instrument to tell you who you are and what you should do. None can do that. If you can stack up your passions on top of your natural talents, you can cut even big obstacles down to a manageable size.

Find the White Space

What you want to do in creating your brand identity is to meld your female aptitudes with the passions and interests that make you unique as an individual. In other words, you need to build a personal brand that best leverages your aptitudes and assets. What's different about you? As Mom used to say, "You have five fingers and they're all different for a reason."

As a branding rule of thumb, when everyone is zigging, it's usually smart to zag, particularly if you are the lesser-known brand. In the 2008 Democratic presidential primary, Barack Obama faced a formidable, more experienced, and better-connected foe, Hillary Clinton. As a member of the Democratic establishment with a husband who had been president, Hillary not only had a strong, differentiating brand position built on experience but was well known (high brand awareness) and, to boot, had most of the deep-pocketed Democratic fund-raisers sewed up (strong brand alliances).

The political race was the equivalent of Coke versus Pepsi.

So what did Obama do? Like a small brand battling against a better-known, more experienced, and better-financed competitor, he zagged. He found the white space his opponent wasn't occupying. His brand idea was "Change" against Hillary's "Experience" positioning.

Rather than going after traditional Democratic fund-raisers and donors, Obama zagged and found the white space there, too. He built his fund-raising mostly around middle-class donors—many were people who had never contributed before to a political campaign—and did his prospecting primarily through the Internet. More than 90 percent of the campaign's cash came from donations of $100 or less. Obama introduced tactics like Obama University, where first-time fund-raisers were trained in raising money and community organizing. Soon, he had a grassroots and Internet fund-raising machine.

BRAINSTORMER

Developing Your Big Idea

Look at the results of your SWOT analysis and explore the following ideas:

My strength, interest, or leverage point:

The market need or problem that my brand could fulfill:

How I'm different from what's out there:

My big idea or brand position in a sentence:

Look at analogy or linking ideas:

I'm a cross between _____ and _____.

I'm like _____ meets _____.

_____ + _____ + _____ = _____

The branding process is simple, but it takes some strategic and creative thinking to come up with your unique idea of what you stand for. Your big idea should give people a reason to choose you and not the other person. You can use this Brainstormer to get started.

Your Name as Verbal Identity

From a branding perspective, your first and most important decision after you nail down your brand idea is the name, the verbal identity you give a brand. A great name can help make a brand, and a bad name can condemn it to the rubbish heap.

Names are important for people, too. I know it doesn't seem fair, because, after all, we don't choose our names. But your name is something you must analyze, too.

Your name can help brand you positively or negatively, and "ugly" names can hurt you. In one study, respondents selected photos of two women they considered equally attractive. Then the name Elizabeth was added to the bottom of one woman's picture and Gertrude was added to the other. So how do you think the voting went then? That's why so many aspiring actors have changed their names. Would Norma Jean Baker be the icon she is even today if she hadn't changed her name to Marilyn Monroe? Maybe, but she'd have had a much more difficult road. Would Caroline Kennedy have made the short list for replacing Hillary Clinton as a U.S. senator if she didn't have such prestigious nomenclature? I doubt it.

The other thing that can plague you is generic-name syndrome. It's a handicap if you have a generic first and last name that are like hundreds or thousands of others. You'll never show up on Google no matter how you market yourself.

✻   ✻   ✻

The best names are
easy to spell, different, and short.

✻   ✻   ✻

It used to be that an unusual first name was a liability. Just ask my sister, Kevin. Yes, her real name is Kevin. And she grew up in the 1960s, when girls had names like Sue, Ann, and Karen.

Today, unusual names are all the rage. Parents mindful of self-branding are spending time and money to choose unusual yet interesting names for their newborns. They're looking for names that are ownable on a Google search.

That's why "baby names" was one of the top ten generic Internet search terms in 2006, ranking up there with "weather" and "directions." There are more than a hundred baby-naming Web sites that offer name databases, online polls, and individual consultations. Like marketers, some enterprising parents are even hiring naming professionals to come up with a distinctive name. What's in a name? A lot.

Most men don't change their last names when they get married, but women do all the time. I didn't change my name when I got married on principle, but all three of my sisters did. Then again, I got married relatively late and had already started to establish myself with my name. Look at Martha Kostyra. She changed her last name to Stewart when she got married, and it was a smart move. Can you imagine her success if she had kept her maiden name and called her magazine *Martha Kostyra Living?*

Some women choose a double-barreled last name. That works best when both of the names are rather short, as in Sandra Day O'Connor or Jada Pinkett Smith. Initials are another option for your brand, like J. C. Smith. Your middle name (Sarah Jessica Parker) as well as forms of your name (Elizabeth, Liz, Lizzie, Betty, Eli, and so on) are other tools at your disposal.

Visual Identity—Powerful

The complement to verbal identity in brand building is visual identity. It's no wonder branders pay a lot of attention to product style and packaging. Each brand aims for a distinctive look and packaging because visual identity can make a dramatic difference in product appeal. A company takes its brand's big idea and name and packages them so that everything works together to create a powerful brand statement.

And the importance of packaging is good for us women since we have an advantage in visual identity: We're nicer to look at! (George Clooney and Brad Pitt excepted.)

Women have a bigger arsenal of tools to work with. Unlike men, we have a wide range of options in clothing, color, hairstyles, accessories, and makeup, so it's easier to develop a memorable personal style that makes us stand out and get recognized as people or as leaders. And having attention-getting packaging is powerful. A lively, colorful package makes consumers think its volume is bigger.

Alliances

Branders also think in terms of establishing powerful alliances for their brands, and you should, too, with people and organizations, with projects and causes.

The school or university you attend is your first brand alliance. Top schools (both private and public) give you a lot of advantages. You have the school brand name that will always be associated with your personal brand. You'll get a great education. You'll be able to network with people like yourself who want to make their mark in the world. Alums will befriend you in a way I find simply amazing.

An Ivy League brand is an edge, but not an overwhelming one. In the 2008 annual survey of S&P 500 CEOs done by Spencer Stuart, only 11 percent had Ivy League degrees.[3] For women, though, school credentials seem to carry more branding firepower. Of the top fifty women on the 2008 Forbes 100 Most Powerful Women list, 20 percent had Ivy degrees.[4] But if you don't go to a top school, have no fear. You'll have plenty of other opportunities to enhance your brand alliances throughout your career.

Education

In school you have a choice between getting a broad education in the liberal arts that makes you a more well-rounded person and getting a specialized education that's more marketable in terms of a job. Or you can major in Japanese art history, as I did, and your focus will be narrow and impractical. That means you'll be competing with dozens of other people for the one job that's available in your field.

I would never advise people not go with their passion, but you should keep in mind that if your passion is in an obscure or low-demand area, then you are going to struggle or else get very good at branding yourself. Like me, most of my graduate school colleagues ended up in careers unrelated to their studies, often after getting more marketable credentials in business or law school.

Although a broad liberal arts education is valuable, you will find that for landing that first job it's generally more beneficial to major in something practical like finance, marketing, accounting, engineering, biology, or physics and study your passion on the side. You'll graduate with more marketable credentials.

But I'd be remiss if I didn't advocate building a strong foundation in all the arts and sciences. If you're an English major, you could be in demand for superior communication, persuasion, and writing skills. If you're a philosophy major, you'll be able to cope with pretty much everything that is thrown your way. Plus, with a branding mindset, you'll always be able to put a positive spin on your background. (If you're on an athletic scholarship, you can emphasize that you learned to be a team player on the sports field.)

It's Your Brand

Realize that the business world has a different set of rules, the kind they don't teach you in school. A lot of women think that the way to succeed is by working hard, and all the rest will take care of itself. That's the way it usually works in school, after all.

It's not that hard work is not important. It is. And the quality of your work and leadership is important, too. But unfortunately, hard work is not enough. I know a lot of hardworking people who are underemployed and even unemployed.

A lot of other factors come into play in the success game, chief of which is "soft power," another name for branding power. I've been shortsighted about branding myself for most of my career, too. I was a victim, like many women, of the good-student syndrome. My mom always advised me, "Do your best, your very best, and you'll be rewarded." And in school, the front-of-the-class, raising-your-hand-with-the-answers good-girl grind works pretty well. You work and study hard, and you're rewarded with good grades. Girls do great in school. It's just that the business world operates under different rules.

✳   ✳   ✳

If you don't brand yourself,
someone else will.

✳   ✳   ✳

If you don't take charge of your brand, other people will do it for you, and I can guarantee that the job they do won't benefit you. You'll especially need to take charge of your brand when you want to make a career change—to relaunch your brand in a new market.

Rebranding

I rebranded myself though several career shifts, none more dramatic and traumatic than my first one. I started my professional life as a curatorial assistant in Japanese art at the Seattle Art Museum. Then I went on to work on a PhD at Harvard, even spending two years in Japan researching my dissertation and translating a Japanese art book into English. So my brand screamed "Japanese art historian."

Then, after eight years, I concluded that I was on the wrong path. So, I decided at the ripe age of twenty-eight to come to New York City and seek my fortune in branding and advertising, areas of interest I had explored as an undergraduate before settling on art history.

Initially, my credentials branded me as an "academic," and they were getting me nowhere, even with the Harvard brand. My negative interview experience changed only after I completely redid my résumé and rewrote my brand story—emphasizing the marketing, PR, event planning, and writing aspects of the job at the Seattle Art Museum and downplaying the academics. Mind you, everything was accurate, but the focus now was on the parts of my background that resonated with the brand I was aspiring to be. You don't have to include everything you've ever done on your résumé, but you need to be honest and accurate as you gear it toward your new goals.

With my revised résumé and new elevator speech, I was no longer branded as an academic who couldn't fit into the business world. My new brand was "promising marketing and communications person."

Think in Terms of Markets

As a self-brander, you'll need to define and prioritize your target markets just as marketers do. If you work in a company, your boss is your key target market, followed by other senior executives. These are the people who have the most power over your brand. So let's designate them your primary target market.

Your secondary target market will likely include colleagues, clients, your network, and your staff. Their thoughts about you will also play an important role in your success. You always want to think "outside in" (what others [outside] need or want from you [inside]), not the other way around as most of us do (what you want to provide to them). For example, how can you be a solution for a problem?

In branding, we say "pick an enemy," meaning, if you want to figure out who your brand is for, you first have to decide who it's not for. Look at the Apple computer ad campaign with the hip Mac guy in jeans on the right and the nerdy PC guy on the left. It's clear who the target market is and who it isn't.

It's the same with people. You should realize that you won't be some people's cup of tea. If you try to appeal to everyone, you end up appealing to no one. The fear of being disliked has driven some women to try to appeal to everyone, and it's a major branding mistake. The "I want everyone to like me" approach doesn't work. Leaders have to be willing to turn some people off. But you want to build a large community with the rest, your brand community.

Some key colleagues at work who are not your target market will be your competitors. Not that you need to dislike them. In fact, you may admire them. You may learn new tricks from them. But you do have to figure out how to compete effectively, demonstrate the special aptitudes you bring to the party, and market your difference. You may even want to form alliances with some of your competitors—alliances are always a very smart brand move.

The Brand Experience

Brand experience is an important concept in branding. Marketers get involved in experience design so that there is a common and branded interaction with the brand at every touch point. That way consumers have a consistent, special brand experience.

Compare the experience of being in an Apple store with the experience of buying a laptop or high-tech gear at Computer World. Or the experience of shopping at a Chanel store versus the Gap. Or having a coffee at Starbucks compared to Dunkin' Donuts. Each company is building a brand image and a brand experience that's distinctive—from product design to retail experience, from the type of salespeople to the bag you walk away with after a purchase. They are creating a brand experience that subliminally, or not so subliminally, echoes the brand's big idea, or unique selling proposition. Take the self-branding test in this Brainstormer to see how far along your brand is.

BRAINSTORMER

The Self-Branding Test

Rate yourself on a 1–5 scale: 1 = bad, 2 = poor, 3 = OK, 4 = good, 5 = great.

	Rating
You can explain your big idea clearly in a couple of sentences so that people know what's different, relevant, and special about you.	_____
If people were to Google your name, they would find you and discover information about who you are and your accomplishments.	_____
You can clearly define your key target markets and the best way to market yourself to them. You know your competitors.	_____
You have a visual identity that is appealing to your target markets, consistent with what you stand for as a brand, and different from others.	_____
You have a personality and a leadership style that are assets and engage others.	_____
Your total score:	_____

21–25	**Fabulous**—You are a brand! Use this book to fine-tune your brand and learn new tactics.
16–20	**Good**—You're on your way to building your brand.
11–15	**Fair**—You need to spend more time on personal-brand building.
6–10	**Poor**—You're struggling to define your brand.
1–5	**Terrible**—Nowhere to go but up!

You create a brand experience every day by the way you interact with people, the impression you create when you lead a meeting, the way you decorate your office, the way you answer the phone and talk to clients and colleagues, the meeting notes you send out. In short, you do it at every touch point in your career life.

Think of all the touch points with colleagues, with employees, with more senior people, with clients. How can you enhance them to build your brand? For example, if you are trying to build a connection with someone new, do you walk him or her to the door after a visit in your office, or do you let that person wander back alone? Are you consistent in the brand experience you convey, or do you convey different impressions depending on whom you are with?

Get Engaged

Brands wouldn't exist without advertising and the media. *Brand engagement* is one of the hottest ideas in media today. Engagement is the process of building a relationship between individuals and a brand by making the brand message and the way it's delivered so personally relevant that people can't help but react to it. And smart marketers try to build strong brand connections at every touch point.

Advertisers use the term *engagement* especially for Internet ads and Internet videos, in which a visual or verbal stimulus grabs viewers' attention so that participation allows them to interact with a brand on a deeper level. Just think about it. The combination of responding to and interacting with an ad or message is more powerful than just viewing an ad.

Indeed, advertisers are even trying to measure engagement using brain-scanning technology similar to what neuroscientists use to study social and emotional reactions. When we are engaged by an ad, clusters of brain cells fire off in the same regions of the brain that react when we experience something pleasurable, like talking with someone we love. So it's no wonder advertisers are starting to use the million-dollar MRI machine to study the iconography of their brand in the minds of consumers. This helps them create the best visual stimuli, messages, and emotions and put them in the right context.

From a branding perspective, engagement is extremely powerful. It's one thing to be aware of a brand, say, by hearing its name or seeing it in TV commercials. That's why brand awareness is the first leg of the brand journey, and marketers measure awareness. But it's something else again to be engaged by a brand, to click through and view a video, for example, and forward it to your friends. (Imagine the difference between being aware of a cool guy in your office and being engaged to him!) It's infinitely more powerful to have customers and prospective customers experience your brand and interact with it when it's aligned with pleasure in their minds. When customers start engaging with your brand, they are likely to develop an affinity for it, and the next thing you know, there is social interaction and your content or ad is spreading virally.

Look at the success of YouTube. Each month, YouTube's traffic is 50 petabytes. To put it in context, all of the traditional media—television, cable, and radio—generate 100 petabytes of content on the Internet every year. So every two months, YouTube equals the content that all traditional media generate in an entire year.[5] That's why advertisers are developing short videos for their brands and flocking to YouTube. No one wants to miss out on the brand engagement express!

Create Your Female Brand

And you don't want to miss out on the branding express, either. Thinking like a brand is a key component in my approach to career success for anyone, male or female, because applying branding principles gives you an edge. But as a woman, you have aptitudes and strengths that you can hone to your advantage, and, of course, you face some societal expectations (some might call them biases) that you have to contend with as you take your brand out into the world.

To succeed you need to create a powerful brand identity—a female brand identity—one that is authentically you and will help get you noticed and viewed positively in the career marketplace. You need to take charge of your brand, your career, and your life.

Explore individual female aptitudes and learn how to build on your strengths. Successful brands, after all, build on strengths and deflect attention from their weaknesses.

You'll also need to deal with preconceptions and biases. Understanding attitudes is core to smart branding, whether for a product or a person. If you understand what people think, you can change perceptions through artful persuasion in the messages (visual and verbal) and experiences you send out. After all, it's not who you think you are and what you can do that's so important. It's who other people think you are and what they think you can do that's so important.

None of us works in a vacuum, just as none of us works on a completely level playing field. But understanding and leveraging our strengths against the needs and perceptions in the career landscape will help us build a powerful personal brand identity.

After all, no matter who you are, your brand reputation arrives before you do. Either you have a personal brand identity that people are aware of or they draw a blank.

NOT A DAMSEL IN DISTRESS

Paula Forman
former president, Wells, Rich, Greene

My mother was one of the women to whom the book *The Feminine Mystique* spoke so profoundly. For her, the traditional female role was sadly incomplete.

I guess you could say that my apple fell close to her tree because I always knew I would have a career. I earned a PhD in sociology, yet I wound up on Madison Avenue, juggling a family, two kids, and a high-profile advertising job.

I don't understand today's young women. It seems they don't want to be like us. Many are willing to drop their careers when they get married or have kids. I would feel terrible if I had to ask my husband if I wanted to spend some money.

I want my own money.

Many women today prefer to stay in safe "women-type" jobs or think the workplace will accommodate them with flextime or schedules built around dropping off the kids. Who would hire them in a competitive industry?

Advertising is a competitive, collaborative process. You need to be available, not on the mommy track. If you aren't fully committed, you'll never get promoted. And when times turn tough, you'll be out altogether. Women and children overboard first.

I was always paid a lot, and for me that's important. I made sure the women I trained understood their worth, and I made sure they were paid well, too. I'm proud of that.

I think a factor in my success is that I took a big risk early on. I signed up to work on a big brand in major trouble at an ad agency. Colleagues warned me that it would destroy my career. Even my husband said, "No man would take that job."

But it didn't work out that way. Working with a strong partner and with my client, we turned the brand around.

I built a reputation very fast that way.

As a woman leader, you have to be self-aware and know how you're coming across. You need to learn how to play it—learn to have some idea of what you can and can't get away with. I am small in stature, and that gave me license to be large in my behavior, to be a charismatic leader.

Women have a more personal style in business, and that's an advantage. A woman's strength is in creating relationships. Men more often create distances. You need to create a personal feeling, a personal style as a leader. That was a big factor in my success.

Of course, on the other hand, you can be too personal also. You don't want to be everyone's best friend. I burned myself out by having five hundred intimate relationships when I was president of Wells, Rich, Greene.

I'll always remember a telling moment toward the end of my time at the ad agency. The CEO and I had some kind of knock-down, drag-out over something. He was screaming and yelling, and it became very threatening.

When I finally got out of his office, there were two creative guys standing there, and I said, "Why didn't you call 9ll or something to try to save me?"

"Save you? You're the president of the company, not a damsel in distress!"

Women can have powerful radar to read customers or quickly sense the politics of a situation. They can detect and read very subtle nonverbal clues to determine who really has the power or how the meeting is going. Women have a knack for getting customers to talk on a personal basis, and that helps build a close relationship. They are more apt to build a relationship of trust.

Elizabeth Hitchcock
Media and Entertainment Group, Microsoft

3

EMOTIONAL BRANDING

Ladies, I think we always suspected this was the case. There is an important criterion for workplace success that has nothing to do with job performance. I am thinking of a measure that seemingly shouldn't even matter at all.

How well liked you are.

Your experience and your branding may help get you the job, but it's an uncomfortable reality that the workplace is a popularity contest, too.

People hire people they like, not necessarily the best and the brightest. Being likable is a huge factor in getting ahead once you're at a company. And women have an advantage. Turns out women are more likable. Studies show that women like other women better than they like men, by far. Men, on average, like both men and women in more or less equal measure.[1] Social scientists dub it the *women are wonderful* effect.[2] This doesn't mean that you can't be disliked if you're a woman, just that women have a natural edge in appeal.

Boost Your Q Score

In branding, as in life, being liked counts a lot. That's why marketers look at a celebrity's Q Score if they are considering someone for a TV commercial or endorsement contract. The Q Score is a numerical rating of a celebrity's familiarity and appeal.[3] People with a high Q Score have strong brand equity: they are *well known and well liked.*

Marketers are looking for the celebrity's likability to rub off onto their brand and create an emotional bond with consumers. Julia Roberts and Tom Hanks are not paid top dollar for starring in movies just because they are famous or are great actors. One could argue that they are not even the best in terms of acting ability, but they do have very high Q Scores, which means they are well known and extremely well liked by lots of people.

It's almost as if the celebrities with high Q Scores seem close to the person we see in the bathroom mirror each morning. We see them as sharing our values and life experiences. We feel a rapport with them, almost as if they are our friends. And the higher the Q Score, the higher the salaries stars get paid for movies or product endorsements.

We've got a Q Score, too, but not the kind celebrities have, that you can find on a list. We're sized up, too, in terms of visibility, personality, and appeal and are compared to other people on these measures. Having a high Q Score will make us more successful, and we can take it to the bank, too.

So, how can you make yourself more likable and appealing?

Create a Comfort Connection

In many ways, brands are like people and people are like brands. An important concept today is *emotional branding*. People buy brands that they like and connect with, not necessarily the brands that they've analyzed and decided are superior. That's why brand personality is so important. When marketers prepare a creative brief on a brand, they often list personality traits or descriptive adjectives for it, or prepare a brand persona as if the brand were a person with a personality and point of view.

Personality is essential for your brand, too. That's why it's important to let people know you beyond the corporate ID. It's hard to be likable when you come across as more corporate automaton than human. Some women, feeling insecure as they operate in a male world, come across as stiff and overly professional. Realize that the corporation is not you, and don't let an overemphasis on work make you appear cold and too serious.

As women, we also have a powerful mechanism for using emotional branding to increase our personal appeal. It's our exceptional power of empathy.

Empathy is the ability to step into another person's shoes and quickly pick up on his or her pain, joy, or other feelings and respond with a similar emotion. It's the ability to relate to someone by finding an attitude of similarity, and when people think we like them, they like us. Most experts in gender research seem to agree that women have an edge over men in empathy. But writers on gender who don't like the idea of male–female differences find the topic disagreeable because they associate empathy with women's caregiving role as mothers. That view is too narrow. Empathy is not only a powerful biological instinct; it can be a powerful career and social tool.

Empathy is based on finding similarities between ourselves and someone else, and this ability is a driving force in human behavior. We are attracted to people who are similar to us in some way: similar beliefs, similar looks, even similar names and birth dates.[4] When people are similar to us, we give them special status, like wanting to do business with them or help them out.

※　※　※

Empathy: Finding a comfort connection
with others through a sense of similarity.

※　※　※

Empathetic people find areas of common ground with the other person by mirroring his or her feelings and actions. Smart empathizers look for things to like in other people, and when people feel that you like them, they like you. We also like people who we think like us. In relationship building, don't look for differences with others; look for similarities. Use your power of empathy to find things to like about them, and you will be surprised at the result.

Wired for Empathy

There's a reason why we're moved to tears so easily by movies. It's often involuntary. Science has unveiled a powerful unconscious mind that processes nonverbal communication, emotions, and all kinds of other unspoken clues and allows us to understand and connect with others. Recently, scientists discovered a different type of brain cell called the mirror neuron. These cells act like mirrors that reflect back to us what others are feeling or doing and are the roots of our empathy.[5]

There are also assessments for empathy, like the PONS (Profile of Nonverbal Sensitivity) test, which measures people's ability to read and relate to nonverbal clues. Simon Baron-Cohen developed the EQ (Empathy Quotient) test, which showed that women score higher in identifying the feelings of others and were more easily influenced by other people's feelings.[6]

MRI and PET scans show that women process emotional pictures through different brain networks than men use. Most women use both hemispheres of the brain (men use one) and have more activity in the amygdala, the core emotional area in the brain. And we have a thicker connection between the two brain hemispheres.[7] In short, our brains are designed for emotional connection. Emotions seem to take up more brain area and have more efficient means of transport. So it's not surprising that women can quickly pick up and accurately read emotional messages that leave men clueless.

And what a powerful tool that is. Women can call up memories with greater intensity than men can. We are better than men at reading faces and can quickly distinguish between facial expressions of happiness, anger, fear, and sadness. We also surpass men in the ability to tell whether something is authentic or artificial.[8]

Women also are more apt to reach out to someone for emotional connection in times of stress. Genes and hormones such as estrogen and oxytocin power our emotional sensitivity and drive our interest in social connections and emotional involvement. Like all good things, though, empathy has a downside. Women are more likely to feel sadness and anxiety and are twice as likely as men to suffer from depression.

A new class of brain cells scientists only recently discovered, called mirror neurons, help women understand immediately the thoughts, actions, and intentions of others. One neuroscientist predicted that "mirror neurons will do for psychology what DNA did for biology."[9] The brain has multiple mirror neuron systems that help with reading people, mimicking actions, reading someone's intentions, determining the social implications of an action, and reading emotions.[10]

The same brain areas that are active when a person feels pain or pleasure also are activated when that person imagines someone else feeling the same pain or pleasure. When you identify with a character on television or in a movie, the mirror-neuron activity that lights up on MRI scans suggests that you are actually living the actor's role and experiencing the story taking place on the screen through your motor neu-

BRAINSTORMER

Empathy as a Career and Social Tool

Test your empathy skills over the next week. Observe the faces, gestures, postures, and nonverbal clues given by senior executives, colleagues, clients, family, friends, even strangers, and ask yourself the following questions:

What messages are being conveyed?

What silent messages are at odds with the verbal messages?

Then try to find a sense of similarity with someone, mirroring the other person and even subtly mimicking his or her movements. Does this help establish a connection?

rons.[11] And it all happens very quickly, in a fraction of a second. It's these unconscious perceptions and identification with what others are feeling that help us understand them.

This Brainstormer will help you assess and sharpen your empathy as a positive career and social tool.

Go with Your Gut

Like empathy, intuition gives you information that you can choose to act on or not. It's a powerful form of intelligence. It gives us powerul abilities in social perception.

Intuition is not some airy-fairy hunch machine but a neurologically based behavior that developed so we could sense and quickly respond to danger. In essence, we can know more through our gut than through our minds. When we go with our gut, we discern what's really going on, not through reason or analysis of facts, but through our unconscious minds. Often, our gut opinion—what comes to mind first—is the best one, far better than what we think of after considered analysis.[12]

Your unconscious mind is a great resource for finding solutions that elude you during the day. Some people get their best work-related ideas while driving, others while showering, but sleep seems to be a great place to achieve breakthroughs. When we sleep, our brains try to connect the dots and explore ideas in a trial-and-error fashion, experiments show, making it easier to bridge the gaps and solve the dilemma.[13]

We all have scanning patterns. Our antennae are up to spot certain types of clues and information. What we want to do is to increase our radar range so that we can pick up more. You'll find that the more you do it, the better you will be and that your gut instincts are often right. Likewise, you can send out scanning patterns to mold a company culture as well. If you're the boss and walk around the halls to stay in touch, pretty soon you'll see a lot more people walking around and dropping in unannounced.

Women are good at spotting a lie, and MRI brain studies show that there is truth to the expression "something smells fishy." The area in the brain that lights up when we hear a false statement is the same area that lights up when we smell something bad.[14] A different area of the brain lights up when someone says something that we believe is true.

❊   ❊   ❊

Intuition is the sense of knowing something
immediately without reasoning.

❊   ❊   ❊

"Leslie," a female executive at a major accounting firm, told me about a group conference call with two other partners and an important new client, a woman. The client mentioned that her daughter had just left for college and then the conference call proceeded with its agenda.

Leslie sensed immediately that something was amiss and wondered to herself, "Gee, should I say anything? I don't know her at all." But at the end of the call she said, "It must be tough being an empty nester. My child just went off to kindergarten today, and I feel a sense of loss, and it's just kindergarten."

Afterward, Leslie's partners told her, "You have just added more value than we could have in building a relationship with this client." The important thing is to have the courage to act on your intuition when you feel something strongly. Use the next Brainstormer to test your radar.

BRAINSTORMER

Test Your Radar—Hone Your Intuition

Before and during company meetings and events with your boss, colleagues, or clients, explore the following:

What is your sense of what is going to take place? Why do you think that? Write down whatever comes to mind.

Look for nonverbal messages in meetings or actions. What are they telling you? Is there a hidden agenda?

Observe Boys and Girls

This feminine edge in social and emotional intelligence—in correctly reading nonverbal clues—begins early and continues throughout our lives. In his book *The Essential Difference,* Simon Baron-Cohen draws this basic distinction between the female and male ways of making sense of the larger culture. Women use a people-based way (empathy), while men use an object-based way (understanding and building systems).[15]

Our empathetic ability starts young. Even girls as young as a year old respond more to the emotions of others and sympathize more. This empathetic ability continues into preschool. Studies show that preschool girls have a stronger idea than boys of what's going on emotionally in stories. Little girls make sad faces and comforting sounds when they encounter a sad story.[16]

Both ways have advantages. Empathizing gives you a powerful tool for understanding people and society. Systematizing gives you a powerful tool for understanding how the culture's organizations work.

Of course, we all have both abilities, but as a rule, women favor the feeling and empathizing route because it's second nature and the stronger aptitude. And empathizing is a great branding tool because it helps you connect with others emotionally. That's what brands strive for.

Emotional Branding

Emotional branding plays a big role in persuasion in advertising and sales. Again, it's the power of feelings over thinking. Marketers try to lock in their brands with consumers with messages that appeal to the heart. Star salespeople use emotional branding instinctively. They are apt to connect emotionally by subtly mimicking the rhythm and movements of the other person to create rapport and a rapid emotional bond.

❋   ❋   ❋

Emotional branding: Differentiating your brand by building emotional connections with your "customers."

❋   ❋   ❋

Just a smile can make a big difference in building an emotional connection. It will lift your spirits and everyone else's, too. (My mom was always telling me to smile. Wasn't yours?) Smiling is a powerful nonverbal social and business tool. Our brains prefer happy faces. MRI scans show that our brains light up when we see a happy face. It's what scientists dub the "happy face advantage," so give people what will make their brains happy and you'll look better at the same time.[17]

Moods, like smiles, are contagious. It's all part of what social scientists call "primitive emotional contagion." Our positive energy energizes others and us. In fact, positive energy is one of the consistent traits of leaders. When we're around positive, successful people, it makes us feel positive and successful, too. It's an unconscious yet irresistible tendency to mimic other people's moods, expressions, and tone of voice, even their posture. A positive attitude is like a seed that germinates success. A negative attitude is like a virus that spreads failure.

Being around winners makes us feel like winners, too. And people perceived as winners get rewarded in our society: with bigger salaries, with awards, with contracts, with important relationships, with board seats. Likewise, negative energy is toxic. When we're around pessimistic people, it makes us want to cross over to the dark side, too. And if we're down, it will be harder for us to succeed. If you exude bad vibes, sooner or later you'll find yourself feeling even bleaker.

Be especially vigilant about the toxic messages you're sending to yourself by saying things like "Oh, stupid me" or "I haven't accomplished much." This sort of negative talk is self-defeating and will ultimately doom your brand. Rather than see limitation, believe it's an abundant world with lots of opportunity for you (because it is). People like positive, successful people and avoid negative people who don't appear to be doing well.

Like = Like

Scientists have been studying exactly how persuasive mimicry works. They're finding that persuasive people imitate another person's movements, even their rhythm and cadence, in a natural way.[18] For example, if a customer makes deep eye contact, they reflect that back. If another customer favors quick glances, that is reflected back.

❋   ❋   ❋

Subtle imitation of another person
produces rapport with that person.

❋   ❋   ❋

Studies show that this subtle dance of words and gestures helps people click. People feel in sync with you unless they catch on and perceive you as being artificial. Persuasive mimicry works only if your moves seem natural and part of the conversation. There needs to be about a two-second delay. Employing these skills can help you get an almost immediate positive response even from someone you just met.

As the boss, what you communicate nonverbally has a powerful impact. In one study, a boss gave employees disastrous performance reviews but did it with a caring manner, and people rated the experience positively. Then the test was flip-flopped and the boss gave employees a positive message but did it with a frown. Even though the verbal message was positive, people felt worse than the employees in the first study who actually got bad news.[19]

Perceptions Matter

When I was a child, my mother always told me, "Don't pay attention to what other kids say."

Boy, was that bad advice.

In business as well as in society in general, we need other people to think well of us. Our success is based on it. Just as in the branding world, everything in the career world is based on other people's perceptions. If people think you're management material, you will be. If they think you're a B player, you will be until you change their perceptions.

We receive feedback every day. We just need to tune in to it. Just look for the signs. Our empathy and intuition skills can help us see ourselves as others see us. We can tap into subtle shifts in mood.

Of course, if you work in a corporation, you're likely to get a formal review. But in today's politically correct workplaces, it may be hard to get honest feedback. Minority women have told me that they don't get good feedback and suspect that managers are afraid to critique them.

But there is a lot you can learn by using your powers of intuition and empathy. What perceptions do people have about you in the workplace? Do people come to sit near you at meetings? Do colleagues return your phone calls and e-mails? Are you invited to important meetings? What kinds of comments do you hear after you make a point? Do people drop by your office to chat?

From a branding perspective, perceptions are paramount. At its core, branding is about tuning in to and molding perceptions and, of course, changing perceptions.

Conduct Your Own Focus Group

Senior executives often get a 360-degree evaluation of how they are perceived by others. It's a confidential evaluation that seeks feedback from your boss and senior executives, colleagues and direct reports, clients, and even your spouse.

It's like a personal focus group.

Speaking as someone who's undergone a 360, it can be pretty tough medicine to read some of these anonymous comments. Most of us see ourselves through rose-colored glasses, and we can crash to earth pretty quickly. There's usually a grain (or more) of truth to the comments, even if someone does have an ax to grind. Throw out the outliers, but look for a consensus of opinion on how you come across. Don't obsess over the criticism; look at the good comments, too, and take action on what you learn.

You can also put together an informal focus group. Take a friend or colleague out to lunch or coffee and tell him or her that you are working on a personal branding project. But keep it light. Keep it fun. The person you've selected should be flattered.

* * *

If you were a famous person, who would it be?
Ask your friends and colleagues what they think.

* * *

Ask them, "When you think of me and my personality, what comes to mind?" "If you were my brand manager, what advice would you give me on improving my brand?" "If there was one thing you would change about Brand Me, what would it be?" "If I were a famous person, who would it be? Why do you think that?" Now, try it with someone else. The next Brainstormer will also help you think about emotional branding.

Bosses and mentors can give you helpful advice on how you're coming across. I was relatively new at one company, and I said to my boss that I didn't feel part of the team that included her other direct reports. Her response bowled me over: "You come across as too perfect, too in control of all your projects, so your colleagues feel intimidated by you."

"Gee, isn't that what I should be doing?" I replied.

"Sure," she said, "but if you want to have a better relationship with your colleagues, show them your human side. Stop by their office to chat. Don't come across as perfect. Talk about how you messed up on something."

Even though I thought my job was to have my act together, I took her advice and started stopping by to chitchat with my colleagues from

BRAINSTORMER

Practice Emotional Branding

You can do this yourself or ask colleagues and friends for their input.

What is your brand personality? How would your friends and colleagues describe your personality?

How could you improve your emotional connection with others in a positive way that would enhance your career?

Try to consciously spread positive emotions through smiling, eye contact, and empathetic listening. Write down what occurs.

Select one or two people and experiment with subtly mimicking their movements and emotions. (Remember to allow a two-second delay.) Does it help you feel rapport with the other person?

time to time instead of just focusing on work. I told them about difficulties I was facing. I even complained about my dating life—nonexistent at the time! And it worked. My relations with my colleagues improved dramatically after I became more human and less work focused.

What colleagues think about you is important, too. While your boss and other senior executives will be the primary ones to weigh in on promotions, positive word of mouth among the rank and file influences their opinion. Plus, you'll find it much easier to get cooperation on collaborative projects.

It's also important to eat a little humble pie if a self-review is part of your company's employee review process. A smart young woman on my team once gave herself a glowing review in a way that left no room for improvement. Now "Joan" was a terrific, hardworking, and talented person. I was very satisfied, but part of the game of self-reviews is to note areas for improvement. Otherwise, you come across as arrogant. You need to isolate some issues, and not the "I work too hard" variety that never seems genuine. Reveal some secret skill that you're working to improve. You'll steal the thunder of the person reviewing you and come across as candid and likable, and the flaw will be diminished in everyone's eyes.

Haggling to Win

It may not be fair, but there are some perceptions about women that we need to deal with. High on the list is women asking for money. Women are notoriously bad at asking for more money for themselves. In one study of graduate students negotiating for their first jobs, 59 percent of the men asked for more money, but only 12.5 percent of the women did. And negotiating for more money paid off. Both the men and the women who asked for more received an average increase of 7.5 percent.[20]

So, women should ask for more, right?

Well, many people—women and men—have a double standard. Studies show that women who asked for more money were viewed as "not nice," while men who did the same were not judged the worse for it. And both men and women who participated in the research had a negative opinion of women haggling.

So what's the message for women? Ask for more money—but nicely? We're back to the double bind. We clearly need to be paid on par, but we do have to be careful about our style, or negative perceptions about women who negotiate will creep in. We can use our empathetic ability to help us know when to push hard and when to push softly. And make sure that you're prepared when you go in to tick off the challenging projects you spearheaded, the revenue you brought in, and your other accomplishments.

While you want to fight for your rights, don't be a gender warrior. Victim talk is a very potent negative brand message, and it won't encourage most men and many women to empathize with you or like you better. I'm not saying that women haven't been taken advantage of, but we may have to see all the planets align before we snuff out all "unfair" gender attitudes. Rightly or wrongly, women hold many of the same gender attitudes that men hold. So a lot of reprogramming will need to take place. Everyone—male, female, black, white, or blue—has been a "victim" at some time. Carrying it around is like a personality flaw, thinking the glass is always half empty.

Building battle lines won't move you forward, whether the charge is gender bias or the glass ceiling. You will be spreading negative energy that will hurt, not aid, your career success. You'll be branded a shoulder-pad feminist or worse. And partnering with men in the career world is a much smarter way to go than engaging in the "battle of the sexes." It's important to realize that many work environments are receptive to women, so if you're not in one, make it your mission to find one. Even consider finding an internal champion among the senior ranks in your company and starting up a women's initiative as a positive force for change.

Leave the Tears at Home

It's happened to me. And it's probably happened to you. We can't and shouldn't stop ourselves from feeling or reacting emotionally.

After all, it's natural for women to express more emotion. Our desire to be more transparent about how we feel about a situation has brought a lot of concerns to the surface in the workplace. And that's good. Women are like the canary in the coal mine, as more than one woman executive told me.

But wearing your heart on your sleeve can be a problem. Crying is generally not smart in the workplace. Women may understand, but men have a hard time handling tears and may think you're not up to the job. So if you feel an emotional moment coming on, it's best to excuse yourself and go someplace private.

Often women react emotionally to a slight in the workplace, as "Melinda" did when her boss overlooked her for a promotion. What did Melinda do? She started avoiding her boss. She was holding a grudge, a bad strategy given that her boss had the most power over her brand and her promotion. Most men realize that it's not personal—it's business—and march right into the boss's office with five points on why they should have been promoted. And they don't leave before getting a timetable for what to do to advance.

✴   ✴   ✴

Don't make the mistake of taking business
relationships personally.

✴   ✴   ✴

Melinda, like many women, took the situation personally. She was hurt and didn't say anything to her boss. She started looking for another job. She was even composing a parting shot to lob at her boss as she walked out the door! Yet, she hadn't done the most basic thing—talk directly to her boss. It wasn't until she resisted those first impulses and met with her boss to outline her goals and accomplishments that she got what she wanted.

Emotional Tranquility

So how do you develop tactics for equanimity? It's especially hard when you want to scream "I'm out of here!" And in tough economic times, it can be even more challenging because everyone is under so much pressure. However, we only make it worse when we hold on to our responses to negative criticism and unfair treatment. The next brainstormer contains exercises to help you stay cool during difficult times.

While you don't want to come across as emotional, you also don't want to be seen as a cold, strictly business executive either. It's deadly branding for a woman. Some corporate women adopt the cool professional image as a way to fit in, particularly in male-heavy industries. But it's a trap, because when you come across as all corporate, it can make it hard for people to connect with you. That's why Hillary Clinton's emotional moment in New Hampshire during the 2008 primary, when she came close to tears, helped her with that state's women voters. They saw an authentic expression of emotion they could relate to. Clinton realized that showing more of who she is as a person was as important as articulating policy and adjusted her style going forward.

BRAINSTORMER

Tactics for Tranquility

Use these four exercises to avoid holding on to unwanted feelings. The first two can be done in your mind in the midst of an uncomfortable situation. Try the last two when you have a quiet moment on your own.

- **The Third Person:** Try to remove yourself from the situation mentally and imagine that you are an observer hovering over the scene. This should help give you perspective and the ability to stay composed. Realize that it's all part of business dynamics, and not necessarily something to be taken personally. People who are really good at self-removing might even smile inwardly at the games that happen in business.

- **Teflon® Shield:** Imagine that you are self-contained, self-controlled, and protected from harm by a nonstick shield. Negative emotions and situations don't stick to you but roll off easily like they would on a Teflon® surface. (Ronald Reagan did it. You can too.)

- **The Magic Bubble:** Visualize your unwanted emotions about a particularly unpleasant situation and imagine putting them inside a big radiant bubble. In your mind, watch this bubble float up in the sky and disappear.

- **The Circle:** Imagine a circle and visualize being in the center of it. In your mind, invite the person who has been troubling you to join you in the circle. Talk to him or her like you would to a close friend. Explain how upset you feel over the situation. Imagine the other person listening empathetically. Then, listen to what the other person has to say. Imagine that you each come to a positive state of understanding as you both depart the circle.

You Are You

You won't be successful building a strong emotional bond with professional associates unless you understand yourself. When you do, you'll be the kind of leader people are yearning for—a leader who will talk to them in a candid and open way, the kind who is willing to admit that she doesn't have all the answers but is committed to solving problems in an intelligent way.

Your authenticity is even more powerful when you have that extra spark, that extra something. In people, it's what the Spanish call "duende." Duende has been described as inspiration, magnetism, and charm. It's hard to define, but you know it when you feel it in someone. You sense their authenticity and understanding, energy and inspiration, like light coming out of darkness.

NOT LIVING IN AN IVORY TOWER

Deborah Elam
chief diversity officer, General Electric

Ivory towers may be fine for princesses in a storybook, but for the executive in the fairy tale of corporate life, I've learned that being approachable and candid are the strengths you need for success.

Although I have many more responsibilities, I feel I am the same person I was when I started out as an intern at GE twenty-one years ago. I think this attitude helps keep me from becoming isolated and losing touch with what's important—people.

Even as a young girl growing up in New Orleans, I gravitated toward leadership. I was a leader in Girl Scouts and the church choir, and the president of my high school class in both my freshman and senior years. But I value most the skills I learned playing competitive high school volleyball: teamwork, networking, strategy, focus, and hard work. These are the same skills required of a corporate exec!

These attributes can be acquired in various places, but sports competition is great training for leadership success, particularly for girls. That's one reason I encourage my two daughters to get out and compete on the ice rink. The other reason is that it's fun.

In college I became fascinated with the broader aspects of society and switched my major from premed to sociology. I still loved dealing with the individual but was fascinated with the macro as well as the micro aspects of society. How does culture evolve? How do individuals form their beliefs?

I joined the internship program at GE while earning my master's degree. I was in a two-year rotational program in human resources. This gave me wonderfully broad experience as I moved from aircraft engines to consumer finance, from Washington, DC, to Cincinnati, to Atlanta, to Raleigh, to Stamford, Connecticut.

This mobility was one key to my success: both the invaluable experience and my willingness to accept new and different challenges. I was single, loved to travel, and eager to take on new things.

Of course, as we mature, these attitudes often change, so it's important to take advantage of your youth. It's normal not to want to move every couple of years after you have a family and want some stability. Today, women need a career that fits us as well as we fit it.

Many African Americans like me took inspiration from Dr. Martin Luther King Jr., particularly his advice to be the best you can be no matter what you do. "If you're a street sweeper, be the best street sweeper you can be." This is true in life as well as in your career. Doing your absolute best builds leadership qualities and shows others that you have those abilities.

Networking needs to be a key part of your strategy for success. Many African American women have a natural skill set for building what I call "comfort connections." We find common ground with people, whether it is through kids, schools, sports, or business.

Most women are also good at cross-networking with women and men of varied backgrounds in varied settings. Too many people think of networking only with people like themselves. That's too limiting. You need to expand your horizons.

Another important strength is that women are great multitaskers. We have to be. We have full lives. We're executives, wives, and mothers.

We're involved in the community. We have to be well organized and able to multitask and compartmentalize.

Continued success, of course, gets more difficult and subtle as you approach the very senior levels in business. By then, everyone is good at what they do. You need to get yourself "out of the pile," as Jack Welch put it. You need to be able to strategically focus on how you are adding value.

Women have often been good at giving credit to the team, but you need to credit both the team and your own role, too.

Success is both micro and macro—yourself and others. Though few make it to the top, those few cannot live in an ivory tower apart from people, who, after all, are as important to the company as anything else. It's important to value all the people you associate with.

When I was made the first African American female officer in GE's history, I received more than 350 e-mails from colleagues and well-wishers at every level in the company. I had to break my policy of answering all my e-mails within twenty-four hours. However, all 350 people did receive a heartfelt, personal, and very grateful thank-you.

Sometimes very bright women tell me, "It should just be about the quality of my work! Not who knows me, or how I dress, or my communication skills!" But the reality is, you're competing with other very smart, talented people. And, all other things being equal, if they are more visible or better communicators, they will have an edge over you.

Rosalind Hudnell
director of diversity, Intel

4

A VERBAL EDGE

There's a big gender revolution taking place on the Web, and it's different from what most of us think. When most of us imagine a high school Internet geek, we come up with a male image.

Turns out that is *so-o-o-o* yesterday.

Today, the biggest creators of Web content—blogs, Web sites, graphics, and pictures—are digitally unconstrained teenage girls. A study done by the Pew Internet & American Life Project found that among twelve- to seventeen-year-olds, many more girls than boys were Web content creators through blogging and posting photos.[1]

Video posting was the one bastion of teenage boys. The kind of videos boys post on YouTube don't favor written words, pictures, and graphics, which the girls use, but rather show off sports triumphs, skateboarding tricks, singing performances, or comedy sketches.

Studies done at Harvard of people thirteen to twenty-two years of age found that teenage girls are drawn to the Web to express themselves, particularly their identity and originality. Indeed, teenage girls are the cyberpioneers of the Internet.[2] Hey, the new generation of women is using the Internet for self-branding! Many cybergirls post online warnings—"Hyperlink and die"—to stop others from copying their material for their own sites. So they're also starting early with trademark protection for their brands.

These digigirls are interested in expressing who they are, using their verbal edge to forge a communication style and connect to others. They are drawn to content areas of the Web. They creatt their own Web sites and visit social networking pages where they can use words, graphics, and pictures. They're creating personal brands and bigger voices through the Web. (In fact, maybe we should encourage more teenagers to have blogs. Think of how written communication skills will shoot up.)

Communication = Power

The prowess we women have with spoken and written communication—our verbal edge—is a tool we can use for career success. After all, a big part of career success is based on this one simple, basic skill.

Communication.

Commercial brands focus a lot of attention on brand message strategy and tactics: what to say and how to say it. And corporate icons, successful politicians, and celebrities do, too. It's important for you as well. It's hard to get the job in the first place unless you can communicate well, even that first job. Indeed, the skills that employers value most—the ability to communicate clearly and persuasively—are skills that new MBAs and college graduates often lack.

Communication is the glue that holds business relationships together. Expressing yourself well is imperative for selling your ideas in meetings and in presentations to large groups or for writing reports, letters, and e-mails. And the higher you go in the professional world, the more verbal agility can help you succeed, and piling on the "you knows" or "uhs" can brand you as not ready for prime time. The one trait most people at the top share is superior communication skills.

Wired to Communicate

As it does with our empathy edge, our brain architecture gives us an edge in verbal prowess, including both written *and* spoken aptitudes. Certain parts of the brain respond differently in women than in men during language tasks. Both the right and left hemispheres of the brain are activated in most women, while only the left hemisphere is activated in most men.[3] Some gender experts speculate that there's a connection between our high empathetic skills and language agility.[3]

Remember, the connection between the two hemispheres of the brain is thicker in women than it is in men. And that's not all. The female brain is densely packed with 11 percent more neurons in the language area.[4] So women are wired to communicate, and how. Our verbal edge is strong across the board.[5]

*   *   *

*Our unique brain network for language gives us an edge
in reading, writing, and speaking.*

*   *   *

Girls generally start talking a month earlier than boys do and seem to use a larger vocabulary at an earlier age. Girls are better spellers and readers. Girls score better on verbal memory, or recall of words. Girls also have markedly stronger written language skills than boys. In one fascinating project, researchers studied two-year-old fraternal twins, each pair a boy and a girl. The twins shared the same parents and home environment and half of the same genes, yet the girls outdid the boys in vocabulary, hands down.[6]

Girl Talk

It's not just the sound and higher pitch of a voice that brand it as female. Women have a different communication style. Because we're empathetic, we may speak in shorthand unless we catch ourselves.

A good friend of mine was working as a mortgage broker in a small office in Vermont. One day, his boss, a woman, stopped by his desk and started a conversation. "You live in Jericho, don't you? Then you must drive through Essex on your way home."

"No, not really," my friend replied. "I avoid Essex because of the traffic and use a great shortcut."

Over the next days and weeks, things got very strained between my friend and his boss. He was clueless as to why. Within three months, he was out the door.

What my friend didn't realize, and later learned from a former colleague, was that his boss's car had been in the repair shop in Essex, and that conversation was her subtle way of asking him for a lift so she could pick it up.

My friend thought the conversation was about driving routes. Guys talk about that all the time. She, being an empathetic female, thought he and everyone in the office knew she was having car problems. And she was furious because he wasn't willing to help her out.

It's the business version of "he said, she said." She thinks, "What's the matter with this jerk? Why won't he help me? And I'm his boss!"

While he thinks, "She's just talking and not saying anything. Is there a point in there somewhere?"

Plain talk works best.

People need direct, clear-cut, unambiguous instructions, like "John, your team needs to figure out and fix the distribution logjam by the end of next week." Vague musings are not the direct, clear communication of a leader. As a communicator, you have a choice. You get to choose whether or not your audience will understand you by the way you say something. As Mom said, "Talking a lot doesn't mean you're communicating."

The female verbal style tends to be more collaborative and cooperative ("Don't you think we should…"). Women are likely to deal with a disagreement in terms that make it easier to swallow ("I can see why you might think that's a good idea, but…").[7]

*   *   *

Girl talk—collaborative.
Guy talk—direct.

*   *   *

Women have a rep for talking more than men, whether it's chatting endlessly with their women friends or not knowing when to shut up. Deserved? No—studies show that women tend to talk about the same amount as men.[8] People of both genders feel more comfortable talking to women, so much so that they are likely to reveal more to a woman.

Listen, Really Listen

Listening is also a communication skill. People often don't listen. They just wait for an opening to talk. So they're taking turns talking, rather than listening when the other person is talking.

But listening, especially empathetic listening, is something that women have an edge with and can excel at with practice. It's very powerful because people realize that we are really listening and understand their point of view. It's not something that comes naturally to most people, so we need to catch ourselves when we want to interrupt and give our opinion. In fact, the ability to really listen to other people—so that each one feels he or she is the most important person in our universe at that moment—is one trait often cited about well-liked leaders.

Listening is also a powerful persuasion tool. Many salespeople are coached to stop talking, ask questions, and listen. And it works.

Find *Your* Voice

As a self-brander, you'll want to capitalize on your verbal advantage by finding your own voice. Voice is about finding your own communication style, one that's authentic and distinctive to you.

Voice is about content, but it's also about how you express that content, even the sound of your voice. You want to find a voice that's true to your personality and point of view, that's confident and says things a little differently than others do. It's not just writing or speaking eloquently, though that's an asset. It's having your own way of connecting with others and expressing yourself. It's not easy to find your voice. Most people do it by trial and error, often combining various influences into something that's fresh and different. That's your voice and point of view.

The words you use and the stories you tell can be powerful and stick in the mind, or they can blow away like packing peanuts in a hurricane. Using a different word or expression slows people down so that they take notice, and it can linger in their minds when they think of you.

Politicians are pros at finding a voice. They want to link themselves with a word or idea that they can own in the public's mind, something that seals in their brand.

A huge chunk of Barack Obama's appeal in the 2008 presidential election was his eloquent use of words and expressions. His oratory and uplifting message transformed him almost overnight from underdog to political rock star.

So words can be very powerful. They're never "words, just words." What you stand for—your policies and vision—is inextricably linked to the words you use to communicate it. Obama was inspired by many others as he put together his own voice: a message about change and a delivery style with a spellbinding cadence, particularly with large groups. His voice marked him as a different brand of politician.

Powerful expressions can even take on a life of their own. Look how one of Obama's refrains in his speeches, "Yes, we can," became a viral sensation on the Web. Millions viewed the song based on Obama's words after the singer will.i.am (a clever brander himself with that name) and his band the Black Eyed Peas made the catchphrase into a song and posted it on YouTube. The video of the song even went platinum!

Verbal Mastery

The further up the leadership ladder you go, the more important your words—and how you deliver them—become in defining your success. Often policy and vision are crystallized only through the discipline of articulating them with your key advisers. You want to define a clear point of view and style so that your vision and ideas are linked to your words and speaking style, and vice versa, which is what marketers aim for in their ads. And you need to make sure that your voice conveys authority and sounds natural. This Brainstormer will help you sound good.

BRAINSTORMER

Enhance Your Voice—The Way You Sound

How does your voice sound to the ear? Record yourself and play it back. What adjectives come to mind?

Try to locate your natural voice. Hum for about a minute before recording yourself. Is your voice too high? Too low? Do you have a pronounced accent or speech problem? Do you recognize yourself?

Do you change your pitch, volume, inflection, and speed to make your talk interesting? How could you improve your delivery?

Leave yourself a voice mail message, one that you are planning to leave for a colleague. How would you rate your message on clarity, brevity, authoritativeness, and emotional connection?

In brand building, your goal is to break through the blur so that people will remember your ideas. Along with naming your ideas and using fresh words and expressions, try to create visual metaphors or images through words and stories. A visual metaphor paints a picture that sticks and even brings numbers and statistics to life. Remember, a vivid visual image can be unforgettable, and stories can be remembered and retold.

Using worn-out words and descriptions will make you seem commonplace. For example, "out-of-the-box thinker" used to be a fresh way of saying "innovative." Now it's so commonplace that when people use it, they seem completely inside the box.

Look at the word *luxury* in the world of brands. Every company in the world that wants the pricing premium of luxury brands has slapped the word *luxury* on its products. The word has become virtually meaningless. It's being used by too many brands that don't provide a "luxury" experience.

The Art of Spontaneous Conversation

You've also got to be ready for spontaneous conversations with both the rank and file and leaders at work. Ever been caught in the elevator with a colleague or even the CEO and found yourself completely dumbstruck? It's happened to me. When you're giving a presentation or speaking at a meeting, you should at least have an outline prepared in advance, so you have a good idea of what you're going to say.

These impromptu conversations can do wonders for your career because they're personal and may lead to deeper connections or at least a favorable impression. So how do you pull it off so that you take advantage of this great opportunity and don't make a complete fool of yourself? Keep up with the news and bring up something topical—a local or national news story (or if you're a sports fan, the hometown team's latest game). Or bring up an important company issue from the corporate Web site. Avoid partisan politics and controversy. Try to carry on a short conversation about the other person by commenting on a recent talk he gave, an award she received, a trade story, or a recent trip he took. Ask a specific question ("How was your trip to China?") rather than a general question ("How are you doing?"). If you think the VIP doesn't remember you, introduce yourself to her and mention what you do in the company.

Stand and Deliver

We all know that when it comes to things that cause dread, dying on the spot may seem preferable to public speaking. Frankly, I recommend opting for life and mastering the skill of speaking and presenting to an audience.

There are three main pieces that communicate and influence people: your message, your voice, and your body language. Which do you think is most important?

If you said your message, you're wrong by a long shot. Incredibly, your voice and body language are *more important* than the message. The message you communicate with your voice and the way you stand and move can support/derail your ideas. Yet most of us spend all our time on the message, not the delivery. We need to reverse it.

✸   ✸   ✸

How *you say it trumps* what *you say.*

✸   ✸   ✸

Researchers have even tried to quantify the importance of each. According to one authority, when we are deciding whether we like the person delivering a message, tone of voice accounts for 38 percent, body language 55 percent, and the actual message only 7 percent. It's known as the 7%–38%–55% Rule, or the 3 Vs (for verbal, vocal, and visual).[9] The next Brainstormer will help you see yourself as others see you and get your body language to speak more fluently.

Perfect Pitch

Our voice brands us as male or female, as high-class or lowbrow, as American-born or immigrant, as leader or follower. Studies show that an attractive voice increases perceptions of your attractiveness.[10] So if you have a lovely voice, keep talking!

An unforgettably sexy voice can linger through the decades ("Happy birthday, Mr. President").[11] But women's voices may be a disadvantage.[12] That's because pitch depends on the size of your voice box, and a bigger voice box means a deeper voice. That's powerful, because a deeper voice suggests leadership and authority. It gives the speaker instant cred-

BRAINSTORMER

Replay the Videotape

Have yourself videotaped giving a talk, in a role-play situation, or making a mock sales pitch. Write down your observations on these points:

Reflect on how this person appears to you based on what you see. Write down the adjectives that come to mind.

Ask others to critique your performance. Write down what they say. Look for common themes.

Study your stage presence: your posture, gestures, eye contact, animation, interaction. Describe what you see.

What are you doing to undermine your power? Write down whatever comes to mind.

ibility. High voices sound unpleasant, while low voices express power. Of course, this works in favor of men.

A whispery, whiny voice or an affectless, low-energy style makes a woman appear weak in an instant and makes it difficult to grab attention at a meeting or in a casual conversation. The high-pitched voice that some women have may be a problem since it is associated with nervousness and excitability. On the other hand, a rough, scratchy sound could make a woman seem more like a man.

Have you ever met someone whose voice seemed to contradict her appearance? The best voice for each of us is our natural voice—not too high and not too low. Listen to your voice on a recorder. How does it sound? Is it too high? Too soft? Too loud? Good speakers vary their pitch and inflection as they make their points. Changes in speed, volume, and pitch keep people engaged in your message.

❋   ❋   ❋

Varying rhythm, volume, and pitch
gets people's attention.

❋   ❋   ❋

Engage Your Audience

Confident communicators often begin with banter rather than jumping right into the meat of the message. Banter softens up the audience with something lighthearted. It signals openness and invites the audience to go on a journey with you.

Good speakers have a conversation with the audience. That means greeting people with a smile and making eye contact throughout. You want to convey confidence, energy, and openness but also *interest* in the people you are with. You want people to feel it's really about them. Move around and use your face and arms to express what you are saying. If you are saying one thing but your body is screaming something else, people won't hear your words. Remember the visual!

You're aiming to be a charismatic speaker who gets the audience aroused. Psychologists use the term *arousal* to refer to the degree of audience interest and engagement with what you're saying. The more arousal you generate in your audience, the more appealing you will be as a speaker. Your mantra in developing your talk should be "short, funny, and memorable." In terms of delivery, planting also helps: planting your eyes on key individuals in the audience, and planting your feet on the stage as you move around so that you take ownership of the space.

Since most women are great at reading faces and body language, clue in to when your audience is riveted and when they are losing interest. You may catch people shifting in their chairs, or someone glancing at a watch. When people stop taking notes, that's a clear signal that no one cares anymore. Don't wait until the audience is snoring. Read the clues!

Ten Tips for Great Communicators

Here are ten tips for performing well in presentations before a large audience:

1. Begin and end strong. To get heard, you need to begin strong. If your beginning is weak, chances are that your audience will tune out. Likewise, in commercials, the beginning is the most important part. The second most important part of a commercial is the ending, and it should be the same for your talk.

2. Be creative. Facts and figures are meaningless unless you say them in a memorable way. Find an analogy that will bring numbers to life or a story about an event that will capture its success. Explore rhetorical devices such as *chiasma*, which is a play on words that involves inverting the order of words in two parallel phrases, like John F. Kennedy's famous line, "Let us not negotiate out of fear, but let us never fear to negotiate."

3. Let yourself be awful. Not in the meeting but when you rehearse. The actor Frank Langella talked about his difficulty in preparing for the role of Richard Nixon on Broadway and said, "Then I just did something that I learned as a very young actor, which is essential: I let myself be terrible. . . . But you know, if you allow that to happen in all things in your life, if you say, 'I don't know how to do this very well, I'm not very good at this,' and if you keep trying, you'll improve." [13]

4. Talk *with*, not *at*, the audience. Disarm and engage them right at the top. I used to begin my talks with what I thought was a provocative story until a speaking coach said to me one day, "Why don't you engage the audience?" She wanted me to break down the barrier between presenter and audience with a question. Not necessarily the raise-your-hand variety ("How many people here have done X?") but, ideally, a question that gets your listeners involved in a conversation with you and your ideas. Or you can use humor about something that was in the news that day to get the audience on your side.

5. Lock in your ideas with a name. See if you can make your case more persuasive and memorable by branding your ideas and recommendations by naming them. Use unexpected or quirky words and expressions, or choose words that paint a picture or position your recommendation vis-à-vis another option. Explore literary devices like alliteration, rhyme, repetition, and assonance, or create an acronym. Chip and Dan Heath, in their book *Made to Stick*, used the acronym SUCCESs to lock in their hook for communicating well: Simple Unexpected Concrete Credentialed Emotional Stories.

6. Be a human, not an expert. Have the confidence to avoid the jargon, stilted language, and overly serious style of so many presenters. Lively anecdotes, stories, and humor will make the audience, even a corporate one, like you.

7. Dance. "Podiums are for principals," a speaking coach once told me. Grab the microphone and move around the stage or the room. Or if you can't do that, at least stand to the side of the podium. Use your face and hands to convey your points. Use a wide gesture with both hands for a major point or successful endeavor. Use a smaller move with one hand for minor points or events. Think choreography.

8. Sing. Change your voice level and the way you present information: shuffle between loud and low for some points. Vary your pitch and volume. Switch the speed at which you speak, too. Slow down to emphasize the important points. Ask questions. Tell stories. Make points. Cite facts. Mix it up. Pause.

9. Create your own slides. Most people use the standard slide formats provided by PowerPoint. But you want a branded not a generic look. Create your own or have someone design a personal brand template. I try to limit myself to seven words per slide or use a dramatic visual. You want the star of your show to be *you*, not wordy slides that everyone will be struggling to read.

10. Practice with a coach. Find help with a speaking coach at your company or on your own. My speaking coach, Tim, is convinced that almost all women speak too fast. He constantly directs me to slow down and pause before and after important words and ideas. I'm still working on my speaking "nicks," like saying "you know" and "um" too much. But you don't need to remove them all, or you may sound rote and scripted.

When It's Awkward

Communicating a message that we don't want to deliver and the other person doesn't want to hear makes for a difficult conversation.

Many HR professionals have told me that women have more trouble with difficult conversations than men. Not than anyone likes difficult conversations. The vast majority of managers say they have trouble giving a negative performance review to an employee. But it's particularly hard for women because we don't like conflict and many of us don't want to be perceived as mean.

So how do you master the art of difficult conversations?

We all have to have them. We have to give a poor review to an under-performing employee, or let someone go during a company downsizing. Or, as happened to me, you have to tell the boss about a major screwup. The trick is to deliver the message honestly and fully—and end up with a more or less positive outcome.

As much as you might prefer to delay the meeting or do it over the phone, difficult conversations are best done in person and always privately. Things only get worse when you delay, because then the conversation revolves around, "Why didn't you talk with me sooner?"

Four Tips for Difficult Conversations

Here are some points on mastering difficult conversations:

- **Compose a clear-cut message.** Have in mind the clear, complete message that you need to give to the other person and know how you plan to say it, since it will be remembered and repeated. Don't just tell someone that the way he is handling a project is wrong. Tell him *why*. It doesn't help to hear, " No, I don't like it" or "That won't work." (A good rule of thumb is to never begin a sentence with "No.")

- **Defuse the bomb.** It's going to be a difficult conversation, so defuse that problem by saying so at the beginning: "This is a tough conversation for me. . . ." That should help set a positive tone.
- **Empathize.** Great communicators have the ability to deliver bad news in a way that makes the other person feel understood and not marginalized. A caring demeanor and eye contact are important. You might bring up a personal experience with a similar challenge and how you dealt with it.
- **Let anger fall like water off a duck.** If the other person blows up, let her vent with this image in your mind. Resist yelling back or being intimidated. Keep thinking of water rolling off a duck. That way you'll remain calm and get the conversation back on track when the verbal tirade is over.

Negotiate and Ask

Negotiating for more money or a promotion is another type of difficult conversation. And women are notoriously bad at it. Most avoid it.

On Wall Street, I heard a woman who supervised hundreds of employees say that the guys start coming in months before their reviews, asking for a bonus. They make their case, even dropping the number they are looking for.

"No women come by to lobby," she said, "and that's a mistake. Because when you are tallying who gets what, you can't help but be influenced. You think, if I don't give him close to what he wants, I may lose him. On the other hand, she never made a request, so maybe I can save some money there."

One of the new ideas is the concept of "investigative negotiation." The key is not to discuss just *what* the other party wants but to find out *why*.[14]

You will uncover more options during the negotiations that may not have even occurred to you. For example, if your salary or fee is the stumbling block, the "why" may be the profit-and-loss budget line. Maybe perks or other benefits could make up the difference.

Of course, you are in the best negotiating position when you have alternatives or are willing to walk. That's why it's important to determine your bottom line beforehand. And to know that if you don't get it, you will have to walk. Otherwise, you will just make a bad deal for yourself.

Asking the right questions can make a big difference. Try "Can you explain how you got to that number?" Understanding why and the other side's rationale gives you valuable information. Another tactic is to say something like "I need to talk this over with my team [or husband or boss]." Stalling slows things down and gives you time to think things over. And you can always play dumb and ask, "Can you explain that again?" When the other side talks more, that often leads to more options.

E-mail: Beware!

I sent a prospecting e-mail to "Sally," a woman executive I didn't know very well. I wrote the e-mail in a somewhat chatty style since we had worked together some years back.

Now, when you are making a business pitch, a lot of your effort comes to naught or takes a while to develop into something. But because I had known her casually at a previous job, I wasn't prepared for her curt, one-sentence e-mail reply. It stopped me in my tracks as I read it. It sounded so strident and impersonal. I got a totally different impression about her.

And it's not surprising. New neuroscience research is showing that communicating by computer is an emotional wasteland.[15] In contrast, in-person communication is rich in content, nuance, and emotion. That's why e-mail increases the likelihood of misunderstanding.

✳   ✳   ✳

E-mail is often misunderstood because you're communicating in an "emotional wasteland."

✳   ✳   ✳

E-mail is something we dash off quickly, so it's easy to lose touch with how we're coming across. It's easy to forget how something we're writing might come back to bite us. Think three times before clicking on "send."

E-mail can have a long life, as many people have regretfully discovered. E-mails can be dredged up in dismissals and lawsuits, overturning your promising career. So be careful not to send anything that might come back to haunt you, like this e-mail from a top corporate executive to one of her employees, which was sensationalized in the business news: "I think about us together all the time. Little moments like watching your face when you kiss me."[16] Once you click on "send," it's out of your control. Use the next Brainstormer to evaluate one of your business communications.

BRAINSTORMER

The Written Communications Test

Look at a business memo, letter, or e-mail and then rate yourself on a 1–5 scale: 1 = bad, 2 = poor, 3 = OK, 4 = good, 5 = great.

	Rating
Make a point: Is the message clear? Simplify things to their most basic form.	_____
Convey my brand personality: The "voice" is consistent with my brand personality.	
Get their interest: Begin strong. In advertising, the headline is the most important feature. Try to begin with a startling fact or an interesting anecdote.	_____
Appeal to their self-interest: Avoid the urge to make it all about you, as in "I want to..." or "I need such and such..." Rather, say, "You know client *X* so well. Could you find out . . . ?"	_____
Don't talk too much: Keep it short. Nothing's worse than long memos and e-mails. Break up long memos or reports with subheads.	_____

Your total score:	**Total:**	_____

21–25	Fabulous—Congratulations on your verbal mastery.
16–20	Good—Work on the fine points of developing a prose style.
11–15	Fair—Focus more time and effort on the craft of writing.
6–10	Poor—Commit yourself to improvement with an action plan.
1–5	Terrible—Make written communication number 1 on your to-do list.

Also, observe good e-mail etiquette. To me, that means avoiding "urgent" flags unless it truly is, breaking the cute habit of using emoticons (those little faces made up of punctuation symbols), and not using the annoying "notify sender" in e-mails.

Craft Your Voice Mail

With voice mail, people can't see you, either, but they can hear your voice, which is a very powerful branding mechanism. Think of how quickly you can identify a friend just by hearing a word or two or recognize a celebrity doing a voice-over in a TV commercial or animated movie.

Take a moment to put yourself in a confident, positive state of mind before you speak. Put a smile on your face as you leave the message. It will make a big difference in how you are perceived. Above all, keep voice mail messages short and to the point. There's nothing more annoying than a rambling message that you have to listen to for five minutes, a misstep women seem to make more often than men. So resist the temptation to go into a lot of detail explaining the whys and wherefores. For example, a good message might be, "Sidney, I hope you can attend the meeting on the X project next Thursday. I'm going to recommend a new vendor, and I know you were dissatisfied with the last company as well. With your support, I'm confident we can get the project back on track."

If you're ambitious and want to take your brand somewhere in the world, communicating and speaking well are skills you'll need to master. The higher you go, the more you will be asked to speak at industry meetings or give presentations to the executive committee or the board.

And when your way of communicating clicks, you'll know it. There will be that wonderful moment in a meeting when you feel at one with the audience. You know it when you're connecting—both the content of your message and your way of delivering it are breaking through. You're looking at them. Some are smiling; others are signaling that they have a question. You can feel the energy in the room.

That's when you'll know what it feels like to be a powerful communicator. That's when you'll know it was worth the effort to develop your verbal edge.

A BIGGER VOICE

Carol Ross
executive coach

"Don't get too big for your britches" is an axiom many of us heard while we were growing up. I think it's especially used by immigrant parents like mine who had one foot forever planted in Asia and one tentative foot (or big toe) cautiously testing the waters of a new world. It's a strange expression. But it was planted in my brain early and is still echoing in there today.

Later, I was delightfully surprised when I found a letter to my older sister from my father (who died when I was thirteen) in which he wrote, "Carol is sticking out like a sore thumb. She got the highest grade point average in her class." He was proud of me! I guess he just never told me so that my britches would always fit.

Being a female engineer is sort of like sticking out like a sore thumb, too. And that's how my career started—working for technology companies. My passion, I soon realized, was to be found on the human side of the workplace. My interest started quite selfishly, really. Some of the technology colleagues I valued were thinking of leaving the company, and I didn't want that. I decided to get involved in the company organization and created a new position for myself around retention. I started programs, like a bag lunch series, so that people could discuss their needs and ideas. I was empowering people, and I loved it.

My career now as an executive coach is focused on creating what I call "a bigger voice" for both my clients and myself. It's what we should all strive for. It's not about ego or conquest, which may be the old model. It's more about feminine virtues like helping people and building community. And community is more important than people realize. It has a bottom-line impact on your business. A thriving community will keep your business going through market changes, and you'll be able to harness the ideas and insights of your community.

Here's an example. My husband's music teacher, Ms. Chen, didn't just teach the piano; she created a community, and that community was there recently when she celebrated her sixty-fifth birthday. Former students came from far and wide to be with her. Some hadn't studied with her for twenty years. Some were now far flung and had to travel by plane. One woman drove from Boise to Salt Lake City to pick up another person, and then drove on to Denver for the celebration. Neither rain nor sleet nor long distances will stop people when you have that "bigger voice" and have created a community around your wisdom.

The path to a bigger voice is using your wisdom to build a vibrant community, to create with others. But how do you do that? What's the right mix of technology for reaching your audience and creating a dialogue? How do you create a brand that makes your wisdom easy to hear and understand? How do you develop new relationships and nurture those connections to broaden your reach? How do you create a community that has a life of its own, feeding on a diversity of viewpoints and resulting in collective wisdom?

Many people have a great network inside their company and nothing outside. The company becomes their world. But that's too limiting. It's a big world out there, and we need to think of the world as our network. So much of what holds us back is made up in our heads about who we can approach and who we can't. What's our biggest fear? It's fear of rejection. I want to teach people that when they are able to connect in a genuine way, without wanting something in return, they open the door to receiving the best that people have to offer. It's a paradox, isn't it?

I feel like I've been on the hero's journey of discovery. What I ache to share is the combination of being bold *and* compassionate, being analytical and intuitive at the same moment. We need to encompass the masculine and feminine worlds in the same breath. That's what I've tried to do using my engineering mind to understand the world and a compassionate heart to see what people yearn for.

My journey is a quest to help people create from their voice a bigger voice.

I call it "The Rule of 3." Unless a group or organization has 33 percent different people, the conversation doesn't change. If there are nine men and one woman, she is the odd person. When there are three women in the group, the dynamics of the room changes.

Graciela Meibar
vice president, Mattel

5

THE BRAND STORY

A powerful way to use your verbal edge is through the power of story. Our stories tell people who we are. When you're close to people, you know their story. And you want to make sure people know *your* story, whether you are an executive, an entrepreneur, a lawyer, an interior designer, or an artist.

A story provides meaning to the facts and experiences of your life. It tells people how you want to be remembered. And story is an effective technique for branding, because the human brain remembers things better when they are presented in a narrative rather than in a list or statement. That's why marketers develop brand stories that wrap myth and narrative around their brands. You could look at commercials as mini-movies or brand stories.

It's the same with people. Telling your story doesn't mean telling everything you've ever done. It means crafting a short elevator speech— a thirty-second personal commercial that defines who you are in a way that's interesting, conversational, and different. It means developing a story line when you talk about projects in meetings or accomplishments in interviews so that what you say is memorable. (If people can't remember your story, it has no value.)

An elevator speech is something you will use throughout your life to communicate your personal identity. You'll use it when meeting new people, pitching your idea, or trying to persuade people to choose you for a different, interesting position at your company and, of course, in job interviews.

✳   ✳   ✳

Your elevator speech:
a thirty-second personal commercial.

✳   ✳   ✳

Never is an elevator speech more necessary than when you're branding yourself for a career transition. But in reality, every encounter is a potential interview that can lead to an opportunity for you. Yet most of us are unprepared, and we botch the opportunity to make a strong first impression by communicating an arresting brand identity. Many of us spend more time planning our grocery shopping than how we're going to pitch ourselves. As a result, we don't make meaningful connections and don't create demand for our brand.

Most of us don't fully use our linguistic advantages as women when we're trying to promote ourselves. And knowing how to talk about yourself—who you are and what's special about you and your experiences— is critical to success, whether it's branding yourself in the job market, lobbying for a promotion, or selling to clients.

Tell a Story

Recently, I was at a speed-networking event for women. The crowd ranged from new grads and MBAs to mid-level and seasoned executives. It included people in transition, those stuck in jobs they had outgrown, and women looking to reinvent themselves in some way. Some were executives, some entrepreneurs, some lawyers, some academics, and some nonprofit professionals. Each person had sixty seconds to give her elevator speech.

One after the other, the women recited a list of what they had done— schools, job titles, dates of employment, how many people they managed, what the company was about—often in chronological order. It came across like a shopping list.

✳   ✳   ✳

There's no brand story *in a shopping list.*

✳   ✳   ✳

Most of the women either didn't have a memorable pitch for selling themselves or didn't have time to get it in before their short time in the spotlight was up. Now, I know men can also be bad at giving elevator speeches, but women have more difficulty in promoting themselves and touting their accomplishments.

For many women, *brag* is a four-letter word, and that's not good because you need to learn how to toot your own horn. Seeking recognition is necessary and positive; if you don't do it, you'll be passed by. It's how you do it that can get you into trouble. You don't want it to come across as obvious self-promotion. The key to effective self-promotion, just as in the best creative writing, is to show, not tell, and the best way to show is to tap into story and the verbal aptitudes women are hardwired for.

Have a Takeaway Message

Before you start to craft your personal commercial or elevator speech, figure out the message you want people to take away from your story. The takeaway message, the core idea or overriding message you want people to take away about you, is your meta-narrative—the master or grand narrative—the story behind the story. It is the overriding idea that all your stories are developed from, and it should be a compelling identity, idea, or message.

For example, no one is interested in messages like "I'm in transition and looking for a job" or "I'm not happy in my current job and I'm looking for something better" or "I've got a business that is going nowhere." No boss is interested in the meta-narrative "frustrated and unhappy employee."

Yet, amazingly, those are the meta-narratives most people dish out when they tell their stories. For example, in the speed-networking event I attended, many women in transition began their elevator speeches with something like "I'm in transition and looking for a job. My last job was . . . " And they tortured us with a very frustrating and unhappy sequence of events. Just seconds into their talks, people were tuning out. That's because the takeaway message was "out of work" and "hapless job-seeker." No one wants to hear that message, even if it is packaged in an interesting story. People want to hear positive messages that

BRAINSTORMER

A Positive Takeaway Message

Figure out your meta-narrative or takeaway message. Write down the key idea you want people to know about you, your career, or your accomplishments.

Draft your support points. Now list three reasons or examples that support your meta-narrative. These could be examples of specific jobs or projects or personal skills.

captivate them in some way, that give them hope about the person and hold out promise for the future.

Use this Brainstormer to develop a positive takeaway message for your elevator speech.

Build Your Story

After you have decided on your meta-narrative or takeaway message, you need to sit down and figure out how to convey the message in a story. Metaphor and analogy are great devices for leading into your story. In describing myself, I sometimes say, "I'm a cross between a brand manager and a business coach." And I might add, "Unlike other business coaches, I'm a personal brand strategist with a background in branding. I use the principles and strategies from the commercial world of brands and apply them to people."

Then I might segue into a client story that brings everything to life. For example, I recently met someone who was trying to switch careers and was having trouble getting anyone in the new field to meet with her. So I told her a story about a Chinese American woman, "Ophelia," who wanted to switch from being a banker to working for a Western luxury-goods manufacturer that was expanding its business in China. By telling Ophelia's story, I conveyed my meta-narrative as a personal brand strategist who used branding principles in an innovative way with clients. And because I did it through story, it was more memorable than a straightforward statement of capabilities.

Disguise Your Message

No one is interested in receiving a job pitch. Just as no one is interested in receiving an advertising message. Or a sales pitch. We're all bombarded with enough unwanted messages daily!

That's why it's smart to study the branding and advertising model. In advertising, product messages are disguised as brand stories in the form of commercials, Web videos, Web profiles on social networking sites, interactive games, events, or product placement on a television show. The job of the creative team is to come up with advertising and marketing ideas that are on strategy, in other words, that convey the agreed-upon takeaway message. The best brand stories often contain very few facts; rather, they convey an entertaining, informative, or humorous "story" that connects with people.

Advertisers select the stories that show their brand in the best light. They obviously don't emphasize deficiencies but instead focus on the areas where their brand shines. And, of course, they may tell stories that highlight the deficiencies of competitive brands. The brand story doesn't even have to be about the product. It can be about its brand audience, their lifestyle and cachet.

* * *

You're not bragging.
You're telling a story.

* * *

Stories are powerful for people, too. As in advertising, your story not only can create visual and verbal connections but also can connect emotionally with others. Good stories engage people. A great story, like a great movie, lingers in the consciousness of the people you tell it to and even transforms the way they see you and the larger world. Stories are also powerful because telling stories doesn't look like bragging. You're *telling a story* about yourself, a demanding client, a team you led, a tough assignment that had a lot of moving parts, a recent meeting, whatever.

Learn the Art of Storytelling

If you're worried about your ability to talk about yourself and your accomplishments in a narrative way, look at the key elements that have characterized storytelling through the centuries:

Heroine. You'll need a *likable* protagonist (that's you). Being a likable but flawed heroine is even better! Think of your audience and how you can best portray the aspects of your story so that your audience will identify with you and your experiences.

The MacGuffin. A term coined by Alfred Hitchcock, the MacGuffin is the catalyst that sets and keeps everything in motion and compels you to take action. In Hitchcock's *North by Northwest,* the MacGuffin is the microfilm of government secrets that the men chasing Cary Grant want to get their hands on. Your MacGuffin could be a global project with a tight deadline that you were assigned after the last manager flubbed it.

Trials and Difficulties. In theater, the obstacles, frustration, and conflict the heroine has to deal with are introduced in the second act. Likewise, you'll want to talk about your experience on a specific project, bringing to life the conflicts and challenges you faced. Use dialogue to bring the story to life. ("Then, at 11 P.M., my client called to tell me. . . .")

The Turning Point. All good stories have a turning point. The obstacles seem insurmountable, and then—poof!—the heroine (you) perseveres and succeeds against all odds. In plays, this typically is the cliffhanger that ends the second act. Sometimes the turning point is psychological, a change in attitude, not necessarily a cataclysmic event. It can be something that you don't recognize as the real tipping point until later.

Resolution. This is the final act, when we find out what happens and the story ends happily or tragically. Of course, since you're selecting the story, share one with a successful ending, particularly if you are marketing yourself. Or, if everything doesn't work out perfectly at the end of your story, there should be an important lesson that you learned. (I remember my mom's words, "When you fail, at least learn something from it.")

Embrace the Struggle

As a woman, you shouldn't have any difficulty coming up with examples of your personal career struggles. But emphasizing the difficult journey, even embracing your failures, is smart storytelling and smart branding, too. Americans love nothing as much as stories about individuals who struggled and came out wiser and stronger in the end. Even stories about projects or jobs with bad endings are poignant and powerful, since we also love redemption stories.

There seems to be some difference between the way women and men tell a story. Men tend to emphasize their command of a situation as they overcome obstacles, while women often have a more organic approach, emphasizing the role of others and leaving room for a degree of luck and serendipity, with one thing leading to another.[1] Both ways can be fun.

✻ ✻ ✻

Emphasize the journey,
not your "victory."

✻ ✻ ✻

Stories that reveal your shortcomings and mistakes are always great to share when you're rallying your team, speaking at an industry event, or trying to talk about yourself in a self-deprecating way, such as when you're giving a keynote address. The audience will love you because you're showing you're human, just like them. And it's much more attractive than just talking about how successful you or your company has been.

One of the reasons stories are so powerful is that they are a concise and memorable way of telling a complex history or series of events. The best stories contain a meaning or moral that isn't explicitly stated so that the listener has to *participate* in filling in the missing pieces. Good stories don't define. They *reveal* meaning.

The best stories reflect deeply American cultural themes: atonement, redemption, and the struggle for advancement. Here are some tried-and-true core themes that can help you develop your story:

- **The Hero's Journey.** Hero stories, like Ulysses, feature a hero who goes out in the world and accomplishes great things. You're a hero, too, when you take on a difficult assignment and succeed.
- **Creation.** Creation stories focus on how you became who you are or how you started your business.
- **Transformation.** Transformation narratives contain a defining moment that changed your career or life.
- **Redemption.** Redemption is an age-old and deeply American theme. Your story could be about your conflict with personal demons or how you fell from grace and then found your way back.
- **Crossroads.** Crossroads stories feature an important juncture where you had to choose between X and Y, the rationale behind your decision, and the impact on your life.

You can also look at female archetypes for ideas on how to position yourself as a protagonist: heroine, female leader, wise woman, explorer, earth mother, or artist.

Learn from Master Storytellers

Recently I gave a talk at a women's convention where the keynote speaker was the historian Doris Kearns Goodwin, an expert storyteller. Now, presidential history can be a pretty elite topic, but Goodwin made it relevant and riveting for the women in the room by telling a series of stories.

Her first story recounted how she became a historian because of baseball. She was a Brooklyn Dodgers fan as a young girl, and one of her "jobs" was to recount each day's ball game to her father when he came home from work. At first, when her dad came home, she blurted out, "The Dodgers won today!" But she learned that when she built up the excitement play by play, she had her dad hanging on her every word, and that's how she became a storyteller and a historian.

Then Goodwin told a series of stories about working with Lyndon Johnson. One day, for example, President Johnson told her that he wanted to meet with her personally, and Goodwin was worried. Johnson had a minor-league reputation as a womanizer. "What was going to happen?" she wondered. Goodwin built the suspense, finally telling us that Johnson's first words were "You remind me of my mother," which brought down the house.

Invite Them In

Goodwin also talked about the conflict she faced as a historian at Harvard University and a mother with three boys. While many of us in the audience might not identify with hanging out with a president or being tenured faculty at Harvard, we could all identify with the dual roles and push-pull between our work, our homes, and ourselves.

After she left Harvard, Goodwin began work on her book about Franklin Delano Roosevelt and his wife, Eleanor, and she told us how she was elevated by the life story of Eleanor Roosevelt (particularly since she felt her own identity had been diminished after leaving Harvard). She regaled us with many interesting stories, including one about Eleanor lobbying her husband to make one allowance for the nonmilitary use of rubber during World War II, the manufacture of women's girdles! And how, at all of her press conferences, she allowed only women journalists. (Since this was a women's conference, that point really hit home.)

Near the end of her talk, Goodwin spoke about Abraham Lincoln, the subject of her latest book, and how humor and storytelling were key factors in his political success. She told stories about Lincoln's many setbacks and early concern that he would die and have contributed nothing to the world and, most important to him, have done nothing to be remembered by. Goodwin had a moving end to her talk, coming full circle to baseball and going to the Boston Red Sox games with her own family today.

BRAINSTORMER

Create Your Elevator Speech or Brand Story

Sample elevator speech about a job accomplishment:

I think of myself as someone who inhabits the new frontier in digital marketing. Recently, I led the launch of a new consumer electronics product called X. We had a miniscule promotion budget—an amount that wouldn't even have gotten us one TV commercial. So we did low-cost videos for YouTube and a social networking campaign on MySpace. To keep costs down, we shot the first video outside a local high school. Things weren't going well. But then a high school student who was an extra had an extraordinary idea, and things started to click and happen spontaneously on the video. We posted the video on YouTube. My client was thrilled when it went viral, getting us tens of thousands of viewers in a matter of weeks. Of course, digital marketing is new territory, and I don't expect every marketing effort to take off like that, but it's exciting working on the cutting edge of viral marketing. That's where I want to make my mark.

Draft your elevator speech or brand story. What is the narrative story line for your brand story? Look for a catalyst that sets things in motion and a dramatic turning point that builds suspense, elements that master story tellers use.

Here's a Brainstormer to practice crafting your elevator speech.

Craft Your Screenplay

When I was a kid, Mom sometimes asked me, "Is that the truth, or are you telling a story?" In those days, "telling a story" meant you were making something up. When I talk about portraying your brand for marketing yourself, I mean using the facts. Of course, it's your interpretation of the facts.

Good branding is always built on authenticity. But no one said you have to use all the facts! You're framing your story so that you maximize your assets and make it interesting to other people. This is an important message, because most women underplay their assets, and it's time for that to change.

All good branding involves sacrifice. You have to focus your brand around one compelling idea, not three or four. And it's the same with you and your personal story. Good stories undergo good editing. You need to leave parts out that will take people in the wrong direction. (Go back to your meta-narrative idea.) Too much information is deadly. Leave out things that are not important or conflict with your core message. Going off on tangents (my specialty) is confusing. You want to have a narrative thread that shows consistent values, motivations, and a sense of self, even if you have made radical career switches.

This doesn't mean your story should be static. We are always updating our treatment of our own lives. And the narrative I use this year is very different from my stories of five years ago. The story I tell to a corporate audience is different from the ones I tell to students or entrepreneurs or a group of all-women executives.

I'm telling a true story, but I'm telling the story that's right for them.

Keep It Positive

The way you replay specific memories shapes your life story, even shapes your destiny. That's why articulating your life and career in a drama is not just memorable branding. It will also help you understand who you are and will be.

There is a strong connection between the stories people tell and their actual life experience.[2] The way we visualize and tell our life stories has a profound impact on how we think about ourselves, how we act, and even whether we succeed. The narratives we tell shape our experiences, so make them positive and authentic but try not to sell yourself short.

More women than men have impostor syndrome, especially the high-achieving women. It's the feeling that you're not good enough and people are going to find you out. We all get this feeling from time to time—that's normal. But many talented women make a habit of this kind of negative thinking. Even when they do well, they think they performed badly. In self-assessments, more men think they'll do well and rate themselves highly afterward. Studies show that men are more comfortable bluffing, or if they know 50 percent of an answer, they'll raise their hands and fake the rest. Many women won't volunteer unless they are completely sure they know the answer.[3]

Changing the way we see ourselves and the stories we tell about ourselves may help us alter our narrative in a more positive direction. Always accentuate the good that came out of something rather than the bad. In studies, people who had sad stories but told them in reverse order, so that the sad story was linked to a good outcome, were more positive and grounded.[4] (For example, say, "I was able to discover an exciting new career for myself as a result of losing that job" rather than "I lost my job but finally I was able to get started in a new career.")

What you don't want to do is tell a happy story marred by a dark detail. ("The job was a great opportunity in a good company, but my boss was demanding and liked to micromanage.") A good way to move beyond painful memories is to think about these experiences in the third person. It will help you reframe and distance yourself from the experience so that you're not stuck there.

*   *   *

Don't focus on what went wrong.
Focus on what you learned.

*   *   *

In telling our stories, we learn what our experiences meant. If you tell stories about your ability to succeed, you are more likely to succeed in the future. Not that you don't have to take action, too, but it pays to get good at recasting memories so that you see the silver lining, since that will help you reshape your bigger life story.

Good stories have a way of coming true if you focus and act on them long enough.

MATTER AND VOID

Edwina Sandys
sculptor and artist

If you were to ask someone to pick the most recognizable name of the twentieth century, they might well choose my grandfather, Winston Churchill. I believe I've inherited at least some of his traits. Like him, I'm ambitious, sociable, and artistic. Like him and my American great-grandmother, Jennie Jerome, I love America, where I now make my home.

Unlike him, I have never been a smoker, but one of my earliest Proustian memories is the rich, all-pervading smell of his cigars.

I came to be an artist rather late, starting off with the usual women's things like marriage and children. I thought marriage was exciting. I felt grown up and loved being in charge of my own domain. I was happy with my domestic life but also felt the desire for a wider stage. I considered running for Parliament. That was the biggest thing I could think of doing. But my husband was already set to be a member of Parliament, and he and his constituency thought they needed me to work with them full-time to help him get elected. I acquiesced and gave up my parliamentary plans, wrote a novel instead, and then found the muse of painting.

I entered the art world at about age thirty and was showing my paintings at galleries in London and New York. Since my work was selling better here, I began spending more and more time on this side of the Atlantic.

Few artists like promoting themselves. And if you're a woman and English, you can feel even more inhibited. Artists think that if you're good, you'll be recognized, but you need to run it like a business, too. I was brought up like most of us with the old notion that a woman shouldn't pursue anything aggressively. Nobody likes a pushy woman, I always heard. Thankfully, that has changed. I remember when I was hiring a housekeeper once, and she quoted me a very high rate. "Isn't that quite high?" I asked. She replied, "Well, I'm the best." Quite right. That's not pushy—that's smart.

An artist often needs to be assertive to get that commission. And the clients expect you to be. They need to be reassured. "That sculpture will be magical in front of your building, and I'd love to create it for you."

In my art, I've been exploring the positive and the void, the yin and yang, the two sides of the brain. I look for subjects that have the in and out, where the empty spaces are important, too. What we don't say and see is as important as what we do. The space you leave empty is as important as the space you fill. In my art, I look for themes that portray this drama. Part of the challenge is taking away everything that is not relevant to what I am portraying. Michelangelo said it best when asked how he created David out of a block of marble. He said, "I just removed everything that wasn't David."

Exploring both sides is necessary to develop yourself fully. If you have children and they are artistic, don't just have them study artistic things. Have them also go into the other side of the brain and do something like mathematics. Toggle back and forth. When you create something, you go into a trance artistically, but as you develop it, you bring in the logical part of yourself. Then, you readjust it and let it fly again. To be successful today, we need to align our artistic and logical sides or have a partner who can fill the void.

As an artist, I want to create work that stops people in their tracks. I want people to look at an artwork as something for them to consider, something to look at, something that will have a lingering effect and keep coming back in their memories. I want them to think how the world is a little different from the way they thought it was before.

I want my work to stay with them.

It's just like having a great waiter or waitress who really connects with you. There's something about them: They're funny, charming, or stylish—they have it! You have to have something about you, too. That special look or spark that makes people feel you are a winner.

Fiona Hutchinson
producer and actress

6

ASPECTS OF ATTRACTION

Should attractiveness matter? In an ideal world, probably not.

But it's not an ideal world, and we're just kidding ourselves if we deny that attractiveness is a factor in success. It won't help if you feel that the world of surfaces and self-presentation is beneath you. Besides, we can all project attractiveness, and as women, we have more at our disposal to do that. Men wear a "uniform" to work compared to women, who can work with a wide variety of clothes, accessories, hairstyles, and makeup. We have more assets and more opportunities to brand with our image. But because women do not have a recognized fashion code, as men do, we also have more opportunities to make mistakes with our visual presentations.

Make the Most of What You've Got

Women in America are often victims of the tyrannical idea of natural beauty. Many of us think that we're either born attractive or we're not. In reality, attractiveness is something we can all acquire. Of course, it's easier if you're young, tall, and thin, but it's amazing what a good hairstyle, flattering clothes, and good grooming can do for a gal.

Consider the French. They haven't cornered the market on attractive people. Yet they seem to realize that all women can be attractive. Frenchwomen understand that attractiveness is about making the most of what you have. And that's a powerful attitude, because attractiveness is a career asset, and everybody can boost her attractiveness.

* * *

Look good—perform better.

* * *

It's the same in the branding world. Branders select packaging and product design that quickly engage a potential customer and appeal to the eye. Of course, you still need a good product under the packaging, just like you need to be good at what you do. But the packaging just makes it more likely that people will realize the product's worth.

You don't need an hourglass figure or perfect facial features to be attractive. Over time, I've made peace with most of my physical flaws. The truth is that I feel better and more confident when I look my best. I find that I'm more articulate, more persuasive, more everything. Even putting on lipstick can be a real pick-me-up. As Mom said, "Put on some lipstick. It'll make you feel better."

Being attractive doesn't mean you have to be drop-dead gorgeous. That can be an impediment, too, since the perception may be that you're not very smart. I've come to admire people who make the most of what they have, rather than the beautiful people, and I think our society does, too. Personal style can transform someone from unattractive into a person to admire and emulate.

Don't Fight It

Whether we like it or not, it's human nature to notice attractiveness. Even day-old babies react differently to an attractive face compared to an unattractive face. And throughout our lives, attractiveness is something we won't be able to resist. Within the first half second, our eyes lock on the attractive people in a group.[1]

So, ladies, while we may not like it, image makes a difference in how we are perceived. Our success in the workplace, as in life, is based on creating positive impressions about ourselves. That's why we have to make some effort with our appearance. We ignore it at our peril.

Two prominent economists proved the beauty premium with a research study based on a mock labor market in which students were employers and job seekers.[2] The "job" was solving mazes.

The job seekers wrote out résumés and, as a measure of self-confidence, were asked to estimate how many mazes they could solve in fifteen minutes. Then they were given a simple maze to solve.

Next, the researchers had each employer hire a small number of job applicants. Some employers considered only the résumés of potential employees. Others saw a résumé and a photograph. Some received a résumé and conducted a telephone interview. Others got a résumé, had a telephone interview, and saw a photograph. The last group got the whole nine yards—a résumé, a telephone interview, and an in-person meeting. (A separate group categorized all the job seekers as either attractive or not attractive.)

The good news is that those with good looks were no better than less attractive people at solving mazes. But the startling news was the power of looks. When employers saw a picture or met the job applicant, the beauty premium kicked in. Attractive people got the jobs, were offered bigger salaries, and were expected to be more productive. Attractive people even fared better when there was just a telephone interview, leading researchers to suggest that attractiveness gives people more confidence.

* * *

"Attractive" people are
perceived *as being better.*

* * *

Both men and women employers had the beauty bias. Another study revealed the bottom line on beauty: good-looking people make about 10 percent more.[3] Like it or not, attractiveness gives you a career boost. And lacking it can derail you or relegate you to the lower echelons of achievement.

The Halo Effect

Looks have a halo effect. When you think someone is attractive, it's like a light goes on in your brain. Because people are attractive, we assume other positive things about them that have nothing to do with looks. Often, attractive people are perceived as more intelligent, more productive, talented, kind, and right for the job compared to less good-looking people. For example, a recent study showed that attractive people were viewed as more helpful.[4]

Your brain draws quick clues from looks and subtleties of wardrobe and behavior. So it's important to tune in to how you're coming across and determine how to increase your attractiveness quotient. Jobs in image-based industries such as advertising, public relations, media, entertainment, and television have always been known for a beauty bias. It's also true for jobs in retail and sales, which involve a lot of client contact. Tony retailers look for brand representatives when they choose salespeople. Some companies even target women who were college cheerleaders.

But the beauty premium cuts across all jobs, not just those in glamour industries. That's why it's necessary to pay attention to it and create a look or style that shows you to advantage so that people have a lot of positive assumptions about you, too—that you're smart, productive, and right for the job.

We can all benefit from added positive attributes, no?

Besides, women have always been stand-outs at creating physical attractiveness.

You Have the Tools

Like it or not, from a Darwinian perspective, physical attractiveness and variety in visual presentation are part of the female route to success. Social scientists draw a connection between the importance of looks for women and our greater variety in physical appearance.[5]

The difference in visual presentation between the genders is enormous. Men have it simpler and easier. Career dress is an easily deciphered formula. They could put on a dark suit or khakis and a shirt and wear the same outfit day after day for a month, and no one would even notice as long as they changed the tie or shirt periodically. If a woman wore the same two suits day after day, that would raise eyebrows. In recent years there has been more variety in male dress and accessories, but compared to women, the male-brand image still is more generic.

Variety and distinctiveness give women a branding advantage. We can choose to wear suits, dresses, and pantsuits. We're not limited to the dark blues and black that dominate men's wardrobes. Imagine the eyes that would turn if a man showed up in a lime green or even a maroon suit, yet women can wear practically any color under the sun. We're able to choose bright colors or neutrals, prints or solids, wool or linen, cotton or synthetics.

*   *   *

Clothes, hairstyles, accessories, and makeup:
Women have more variety for crafting their visual brand.

*   *   *

Most men add a dash of individuality with just a tie or, in a casual workplace, a shirt. But we have our accessories: earrings, necklaces, and bracelets, not to mention handbags and shoes. All these items make us attractive and distinct from other women—more branded. Granted, some men are into stylish clothes, jewelry, or tattoos, but as a rule, most aren't and tend to have a narrower range of clothes, jewelry, shoes, and the like and to own fewer items. The vast difference between the ways men and women approach appearance includes the wide range of hairstyles and makeup women sport compared to men.

Under the Microscope

In our visual age, we've become obsessed with the way things look. And no one gets dissected and scrutinized more than women. When prominent businesspeople and professionals are under the floodlights, it's the women who get the most scrutiny on their looks and appearance.

You can be the CEO of a Fortune 100 company, and, inevitably, if you're a woman, a reporter is bound to ask, "Who designed the suit you're wearing?" In the news story, you'll likely find a description of your clothes, your hair, and your jewelry. And if you're a high-profile woman, be prepared to be examined by scores of media sibyls.

Since we're going to be scrutinized more, why not use it to our advantage? Why not dress to telegraph our brand message? Why not package ourselves as a premium brand? We can dress to inspire and project authority but in a softer more approachable way. Look at Diane Sawyer—she avoids trendiness but looks stylish and strong. She looks appropriate, but not overly cautious as a dresser. She looks like her own woman. She looks like a winner.

For women, there's a double bind with the way we look, so it pays to heed the unwritten style rules we have to learn to be successful in the professional world:

• Be attractive but not glamorous.
• Be feminine but not sexy.
• Be strong but not severe.
• Be stylish but not trendy.

It's not easy, because if we come across as too soft and feminine, people will wonder if we're tough enough for the job, and if we come across as too tailored and masculine, they won't want us in the job because we're too tough.

All these snap judgments happen quickly, in just a fraction of the first second: attractive or unattractive, hire or don't hire, successful or loser. They're based on flash visual impressions: how you look, your clothes, your hair, your posture, even the way you inhabit space.

People won't really hear what you say until they've sized up your visual identity. And we're all guilty of making these snap judgments based on a person's appearance. Social scientists talk about thin-slicing, the ability to see something for a few seconds and form a very accurate impression about it.[6] Incredibly, that blink-of-an-eye impression usually matches the opinion we have after considered analysis. New research shows that we don't even need a full second to grasp something. Just a *microthin* slice—in some studies, just *two-tenths of a second*—is enough time for a person to take some-thing in and evaluate it.[7] So be prepared. (As Mom said, "Half the battle is looking successful.") The next Brainstormer offers a self-image assessment.

Fashion Is Ideas

Taking an interest in clothes can seem frivolous or bourgeois, girly or nonintellectual. Many successful career women I know think that talk of clothes and fashion is beneath them. As someone once said to me, "No thoroughbred was ever a clotheshorse." But you don't have to be an avid reader of *Vogue* or even take an interest in fashion to build a wardrobe that helps you communicate your brand message.

Look at how first Lady Michelle Obama sends messages with her clothes. Her choices of immigrant designers subtly telegraphs multicul-turalism and the quest for the American dream, core themes in the pres-ident's speeches.[8] At the inauguration in 2009, the new first lady dressed

BRAINSTORMER

Do a Self-Image Assessment

How would you describe your visual identity and image?

What do you *want* your entire package to say about you? Is it consistent with *your* personal brand strategy?

What is your best feature? How can you play it up more?

What is your worst feature? How can you minimize that feature?

What distinctive features do you have? Which of your features are different from those of other people? How could you accentuate the difference?

How would you describe your clothing style? Do you have one? Is it consistent?

her daughters not in designer duds, but in J. Crew so that they appeared accessible to the average American.

Fashion is a balancing act. You don't want to look like you're obsessed with clothes and neglect your mind. But playing it too safe and proper says that you're insecure and dull. It's all about interpretation.

Perhaps because the pairing of women and power is relatively new, dress may be a danger zone for female executives. Heaven forbid, if you play it too downscale or too sexy, you could be a liability to your company. In fact, two image consultants I know get steady business from corporate executives who don't want to confront female employees with their fashion faux pas and hire consultants to do the dirty work.

Clothes won't make a big difference in how well you do your job, but they can make you feel better about yourself, which always helps, particularly in tough situations. The right clothes will have a significant effect on what people think about you on the job. Clothes are a quick read, a symbolic language, one of the easiest ways to communicate information about who you are. In many ancient cultures, clothing was very precise. You could look at people and tell the class they belonged to by the color, style, and motifs of their clothes. In our society today, people judge us by our clothes and how we put ourselves together, just as in those ancient cultures.

Office Attire

For a career woman, dressing appropriately is a business skill. It speaks to your judgment and will affect your credibility. So while you may be a believer in freedom of expression, looking like part of the clique in *Sex and the City* could hamper your career aspirations unless you work in the fashion industry in New York. But don't get hung up on hard-and-fast rules for corporate dressing. It's silly to insist, as some image consultants have, that senior women should wear light-colored suits so that they'll be less intimidating, or that women should restrict themselves to tailored, collared jackets, like men, or avoid dresses because the garments are too feminine. We're beyond that, I hope. The right kind of dress can work wonderfully well in the workplace.

As you put together your career look, much depends on what you do and where you work. Some women make the mistake of wearing clothes that are too casual or send the wrong brand message. So if you're thinking that you'll just wear some old pants and a cardigan on a day when you don't have to meet with any clients, think about your office colleagues. Don't they matter? After all, some of them have a lot of power over your brand in terms of promotions and pay. Now, if you're a one-woman business working out of your home, that's a different story (although it could affect your opinion of yourself).

Then there is the other extreme, sexy attire that's too short, too tight, too revealing and sends the signal that you're a better dinner date than a business colleague.

Look the Part

For most career women, there's one thing you must do with your image. You must project authority.

If you work in a corporate job, you can get ideas on how to project authority with your clothes by looking at what female politicians (think Nancy Pelosi) and news anchors (look at Katie Couric or your local television anchors) wear.

Women in the public eye are under so much surveillance that you can take advantage of the feedback they receive daily. They are good barometers of what works in terms of clothes, hairstyles, and jewelry for women of substance. But you don't want to copy someone. You want to create your own brand look. When Arianna Huffington started appearing on TV, she noticed that all the other women were wearing suits with shirts underneath. "But I thought, 'Why do we all have to look like men?'" Huffington explained, and she opted for something that wasn't a suit. By choosing feminine blouses and dresses, she makes a statement that's feminine yet strong. "I also have a limited color palette," she added. "But this way who you are and what you say can be the focus rather than your red suit or green jacket."[9]

Look also at what successful women in your organization wear. Not that you are going to clone their wardrobes, but if your goal is to rise in the organization, you need to look like someone who could be invited to the executive floor. You might even get a store expert or a personal image consultant to help you put together a look that conveys the brand image to which you aspire and is also distinctive and suited to you. From a branding perspective, you have an opportunity to really make your mark. Find a few designers whose clothes work for you and concentrate on them.

If the dress code in your company is formal attire for the senior executives and casual attire for the rank and file, mix both business casual and formal business attire as your regime. Keep a jacket at the office. Then if an unexpected client meeting comes up, you won't be excluded. But even though so many senior executives never dress down, that doesn't mean things haven't loosened up. Take pantyhose. There's a raging debate in some offices about whether you can toss them in the dustbin and go bare legged, an act that would have caused heads to turn not too long ago. So you have to figure out what's right for the culture where you work.

Don't be the most casually dressed person in your company. Casual Friday is easy for the guys: it's khakis and a shirt. For ladies, it's a skirt and blouse, a dress, or nice pants. Don't wear jeans, shorts, T-shirts, or flip-flops, except to the company beach party or barbeque, or jogging pants, unless it's the corporate charity run. On the West Coast, where things are more casual, take your cue from what the more senior women are wearing.

Be in Sync

A job interview is the time to make sure that the message you're convey-ing is pitch-perfect. People are making hiring decisions based on little information, so the way you look takes on increased importance. Put as much effort into planning your wardrobe as you do into planning your answers to interview questions. For example, take "Amelia," who wore her best power suit for a job interview at a start-up merchandiser. She clicked with the two young entrepreneurs who had started the enterprise, but she did notice that everyone was casually dressed. For her callback interview, Amelia played it safe by choosing another power suit. But it turned out to be the wrong thing to wear, and the feedback she got when she was dropped from the list of contenders was that the founders felt she was too corporate and wouldn't fit in with a hands-on start-up.

The area that often goes haywire for women is evening events. It's one thing if an administrator wears a plunging neckline to a business event, but if a mid-level or senior woman does it, tongues will wag. You might think you're just being liberated or stylish like the celebrities we see walking the red carpet, but exposed skin sends signals to men that you may not intend. After all, the area of the brain pertaining to sexual pursuit is twice as large in men, and that's not the part of the male brain you want to stimulate at work.[10]

That's You!

A signature accessory or color can be a smart branding device for Brand You. Your trademark could be unusual combinations of jackets and pants. For example, Sarah Palin uses unusual glasses as a branding statement. It could be a fabulous necklace collection that is always part of your wardrobe. Or it could be a color or color palette that you adhere to religiously—brands think of owning a color.

Here's a short Brainstormer to get you thinking of a more personal and identifiable look.

BRAINSTORMER

Develop a Branded Look

Do you have a consistent and personal style of dressing that people associate with you? If so, what is it? If not, what style is appropriate for your brand?

Do you have a signature item or accessory that's different? If so, what is it? If not, what would be appropriate for your brand?

Your business card is part of your visual identity, too, and the company-issue business card is very corporate and generic in appearance. Many women are dumping the corporate cards outside of official business in favor of personal calling cards that are beautiful and distinctive. Your custom-made business card is the perfect thing to use for non-company-related activities and social occasions.

Often these cards are stylishly elegant, with a simple graphic mark or monogram in color and no contact information whatsoever. That way you can write in what you think is appropriate for each person, making it highly individualized. Or you can have the minimum: name, e-mail, and phone (either your direct line or your assistant's). Carry your personal cards in a special card case and have a nice pen—it's all part of your branding. Think about presentation and spend some time on the format of your other business marketing materials, like your résumé. You could add corporate logos in color next to the company names in your job experience list; they would stand out and contribute visual appeal to the document.

Do Something with Your Hair

Hair is a powerful branding device, especially for women. Think of what her stiff helmet hairstyle says about Queen Elizabeth II. Or what Katie Couric's chin-length modern bob says about her. Or the impression you convey if you're stuck in a hairstyle reminiscent of Alice in Wonderland.

It's as if there are hair police who have it out for women. As Dee Dee Myers, the first female presidential press secretary, said, "People don't hear a word you say until they get over your hair."[11] For women, unfortunately, gray hair is aging and could hurt your career. An actress friend with wonderful silver hair asked me if she should color her hair. The problem? She's being cast in roles that call for a sixty-five-year-old woman, and she's only in her early fifties. If she wants younger parts, the answer is yes.

Your Body Talks

The first impression you make is the most powerful and the most lasting. How do you enter a room? Do you stand tall and walk purposefully? Or do you slouch and look distracted? Do you come across as tired? Or stressed?

A lawyer friend told me that she revs up before entering the courtroom by taking a brisk walk outside (or down the corridor), to get her energy level up, then stands tall and enters the courtroom very slowly and confidently. Interestingly, just improving your posture boosts your self-esteem.

It also pays to have an animated face. We looked at the "happy face advantage" in chapter 3, and research shows that women are more animated than men. Those nods and smiles contribute positively to attractiveness.[12] Effective politicians are always doing this.

Look Beyond Looks

Attractiveness is a many-faceted thing. It includes appearance, grooming, and personal style, but it goes way beyond your looks. It's hard to find a single measure of attractiveness, and a lot of attractiveness clearly is not facial beauty but being pleasant and looking healthy, relaxed, and fit. So adopting a weekly exercise routine and getting enough sleep can do wonders for your appearance. (Not to mention everything else.)

Personality can make someone a person to admire and emulate. Attractiveness is also your character, your charisma, the sound of your voice, the way you stand and move, the way you write, even your wit and humor. All these things send branding messages. They reflect who you are on the inside.

Many of the things that make up attractiveness are not expensive— not that they don't entail some effort. The next Brainstormer should make it easier for you.

BRAINSTORMER

Increase Your Attractiveness Quotient

Look at all your visual assets—hair, eyes, posture, figure, face, energy, hands. How can you maximize them?

Look at other components of attractiveness, such as personality, a healthy aspect, relaxed confidence, and positive energy. How could you increase your attractiveness quotient?

Look at executive presence—your body language, your posture, the way you walk and move—as a part of attractiveness. How can you improve?

Attractiveness is also projecting confidence, being comfortable in your own skin. It's in the way you inhabit space, even in how you move. Look at Marilyn Monroe. She's become an icon not just because she was considered beautiful (after rebranding herself by changing her name from Norma Jean Baker and bleaching her hair). Many contemporaries felt that she had the perfect body measurements (37C-23-36, in case you wanted to know), giving her an ideal waist-to-hip ratio (0.64).

Monroe's attractiveness also came from the way she moved. Sure, she had a lovely face and figure, but she paired these assets with a pronounced hip sway or practiced sashay.[13] She was careful to exploit this any time she was "on" as Marilyn. If she had moved with a lumbering gait or been awkward, she wouldn't have appeared beautiful.

Flirting? No.

Ever since Adam and Eve, putting men and women together has been bound to create some sparks. But there's a difference between engaging in mild friendly flirtation and being labeled flirtatious.

Mild flirtation is the kind that lets a male colleague know "I think you're funny" or "I think you're cool." Being flirtatious carries more than a hint of sexuality and almost always backfires in the workplace, usually on the woman. One study showed that women MBAs who were flirtatious got fewer promotions and earned less than their peers who did not flirt.[14] In another study, people were shown two separate videos. In one, women displayed flirtatious behavior, like batting their eyes and flipping their hair, and wore short skirts and tops with low necklines. In the other video, women wore conservative pantsuits and had straightforward behavior. Both groups had similar résumés. You guessed it. The flirtatious women got lower scores in leadership and job capability.

Even if you're not being flirtatious, think about what your clothes are saying at dressy business functions. If you find male executives staring at your décolletage, not your face, you're wearing the wrong dress.

Forever Young

It's going to happen to you. And it's already started to happen to me.

If you're like me, it's a subject you don't like to talk about, but you think about it more than you want to admit.

Aging.

*   *   *

Age is not an asset for women.

*   *   *

Anne Bancroft was only thirty-six when she portrayed the older woman, Mrs. Robinson, in *The Graduate.* And Dustin Hoffman, who was just six years younger, played someone her daughter's age!

Feeling depressed yet?

It's important to have a realistic attitude about aging because being older is a particular liability in the workplace for women. Gray-haired men can have a wise avuncular quality that's appealing to the highest levels. Few women are perceived as the office sage.

There's a lot to be said for aging gracefully. But you still need to look contemporary and like a player, so I'm all for trying to dial time back a bit by camouflaging gray hair and ditching the matronly clothes or matchy-matchy suits for contemporary styles that work with your age.

Ten Tips for Bridging the Beauty Gap

OK, so you aren't a natural beauty. Neither am I. But we can still succeed. Here are ten tips for bridging the gap:

1. Have fun and create a *personal look.* Dressing should be fun and express who you are. Find your own vibe—a look you're comfortable in—that makes you *feel* good and doesn't get in the way of working. Aim for a trademark look that's distinctively you and that people associate with you, but realize that your look can include couture pieces paired with something from H&M or Target.

2. Remember, likability trumps looks anyway. Your personality and spirit are an important part of being attractive. Smile and make eye contact. An open, positive attitude exudes energy and makes you more likable. Put the focus on other people. Like them, and they will like you and be attracted to you.

3. Don't neglect your hair. Hair is a powerful branding device for women. Your hair frames your face, so get a cut and a style that work with your face and don't distract from your personal brand message.

4. Have a visual trademark. Find a signature accessory that jumps out and that people associate with you. It could be your glasses, your handbag, or distinctive jewelry. It could be a color that defines you. Don't limit yourself to the color the fashion magazines are promoting for the season, either. Use your trademark consistently so that people associate it with you.

5. Project positive body language. Have you noticed how many people walk around with frowns on their faces? Or shuffle along with a slump? You knock people over with these nonverbal messages every day, so make them positive messages. Good posture alone can improve your self-esteem and attractiveness.

6. Cultivate your voice. Have you ever met someone whose voice did not seem to match his or her appearance? A good voice enhances your looks, and a bad one detracts from your attractiveness.

7. Don't follow the fashionistas. Don't get the "it" bag or the "must have" anything, or you'll look like a follower, not a leader. It's a sign of insecurity. Tip your hat to style but select something surprising, not the obvious choice.

8. Be comfortable and relaxed. You need to look relaxed in the way you dress and carry yourself. A gym routine helps you project health and can produce dramatic changes in how people perceive your looks. You don't need an hourglass figure, either, just a healthy, relaxed attitude.

9. Look real. Looking real is integral to style and attractiveness. So go easy on the makeup and accessories. Nothing ages a woman more than desperately trying to look young.

10. There are no rules except to look groomed and appropriate.
As Mom said, "If your hair looks good and you have good shoes that go with the outfit, you're 70 percent there." But there are no hard-and-fast rules. A fashion maven of a certain age known for her dramatic style told me of a visit to a top shop in London. "How old do you have to be to stop wearing vintage?" a woman asked her. She said, "How old do you have to be to stop wearing clothes?"

WOMEN:
THE ROAD TO SUCCESS

Joi Gordon,
CEO, Dress for Success

Most people want to fit in, but ever since I was a child, I have wanted to be different and to be remembered. It wasn't difficult to do that growing up as an African American in Tulsa, Oklahoma. I was always starting things—the first black woman to do this or the first black woman to do that. For me, being part of a minority was an opportunity to stand out. It was a great experience. I went to college and law school without student loans. I finished seven years of college owing nothing.

When I came to the Bronx to be a criminal attorney, it was the first time in my life that I didn't stand out. I was one of many.

I couldn't figure out how I could stand out until I was watching TV one day. I saw a segment on Dress for Success, an organization helping women get clothes so they could get good jobs. I went in to donate some suits, and I met the founder, Nancy Lublin, who had started the organization with a $5,000 inheritance she had received from her great-grandfather. Within sixty days I was asked to join the board, and four years later I was running the worldwide organization. I had found my passion.

The premise of Dress for Success is women helping other women. I think women are wired to help other women. For women, self-confidence is very linked to the image we have of ourselves. If you don't have the appropriate clothes, you're not going to be able to do your best at the job interview. We make it easy for women all over the United States and all over the world to be a part of other women's career journey. Although we're best known for giving out suits, we want to be known for keeping women employed. That's why we have mentoring, coaching, and seminars—all the tools women need to land a job and be successful.

We're still a midsize nonprofit, so I tend to do a little bit of everything and try to do a lot with less. It could be easy to burn yourself out because there is so much to get done.

I meet with many corporate women who are interested in moving into a nonprofit job. They've made good money, but they don't feel satisfied. They don't feel fulfilled. At the executive level, nonprofits are often looking for advanced degrees: a master's or PhD. If there is a strong counseling component, it may be important to have an MSW. Many of us in the nonprofit community joined a nonprofit when it was small and had little funding and worked hard to build it into what it is today. So there can be skepticism about someone's commitment and whether they, too, would have worked as hard. I definitely think there is something to be gained for nonprofits from individuals with for-profit business backgrounds. I think all you need to see in a candidate is passion coupled with talent.

It's one thing to have a job, and quite another to love what you do. My job completely changed my life. I love coming to work. I feel that I'm helping to change the world.

Like my organization, my personal brand is about women helping other women. The women on my board, they allow me to stand on their shoulders. I've felt nothing but love from these women. For me, mentoring and networking is about helping others. How can I help you?

I feel lucky to be paid for getting and giving joy (just like my name).

Women wait to be asked, but maybe no one asks. You need to volunteer for big assignments. Raise your hand! Take some risks!

Billie Ida Williamson
partner, Ernst & Young

7

THE FEMALE STYLE OF LEADERSHIP

Imagine that you and your team are working on a difficult project with a tight deadline. You brought together a varied crew to kick around solutions. You recruited junior and senior people from your group. You even invited some outside people from other departments so you could get their perspectives.

Some of the ideas are intriguing. Some are off the wall. Some are uninspired. But a junior person we'll call Bronwen came up with a terrific solution.

You're the leader who will be presenting the recommendation to top management. Do you take credit? Or do you say, "This idea actually came from a junior team member—Bronwen"?

Give Recognition, Get Loyalty

You could take full credit for yourself, as some leaders do. Who would blame you? (It's a dog-eat-dog world, isn't it?) You paid your dues slogging it out in the trenches, right? After all, you're on the hook when things tank.

That could be one way to act. Just not the best way.

While there is often little difference between the sexes in leadership studies, women seem to favor a leadership style that is more democratic, one founded on collaboration, teamwork, and recognition.[1] More people are empowered to contribute and are recognized for it. It's a way of leading that fosters loyalty to the leader and goodwill with the rank and file.

It's easy to understand why. Praising top-notch contributors and recognizing the creators and the doers regardless of status is the "carrot principle" in action. By giving recognition, you engage all the members of your team and give them credibility with higher-ups and clients. When you demonstrate that you value others, they will value you. It's a classic win-win.

It's a more personal leadership style. This way of leading says that you value people, that you reward individual contributions and potential, that you're fair and more accessible. And this will come back to benefit you. After all, leadership is about hope. It's about the belief that, with you at the helm, things will be better and obstacles will be surmounted. If people believe that you are going to help them have a better future, they will rally around you and get the work done. And you will attract willing and enthusiastic followers and clients.

A meta-analysis of female and male leadership styles led by Professor Alice Eagly, which looked at forty-five leadership studies, found that women tend to create a different brand experience and way of engaging with others.[2] Women are slightly more likely than men to be "transformational leaders" who seek to inspire, like a mentor or a coach. They tend to nurture and empower employees and encourage teamwork and innovation by collaborating more with people and sharing decision making. They are likely to praise and reward when projects exceed expectations.

As leaders, women have more of a big-picture orientation. They are also more intuitive in their approach to decision making and more personal in their leadership style. Of course, having a mentoring leadership style has its drawbacks, too, if you spend too much time mentoring others and success at your organization is based on other measures.

In contrast, men tend to be "transactional leaders" who tend more toward a command-and-control style and set up an exchange-type rela-

CHARACTERISTICS OF THE FEMALE LEADERSHIP STYLE

- Acting as a mentor, coach, or team leader
- Collaborating and sharing the decision making
- Being more subjective and consensus driven
- Nurturing and empowering employees
- Having a strong people orientation
- Encouraging ideas from all levels

tionship with employees. Interestingly, women did score higher than men in one area of transactional leadership: rewarding employees for good performance. [3] Use the Brainstormer to see which leadership camp suits your nature.

So why do more women tend to gravitate toward a more inclusive team-leader approach? Some think it may be a safer bet for women because they won't seem bossy. But the traits of the female leadership style also show up in childhood studies of boys and girls. When asked to solve a problem, girls are more likely to form teams and collaborate on decisions, while boys are more apt to appoint a leader who gives orders.

Now for the disclaimer. We are all different. Some of us have a more feminine style, some a more masculine style, and others an integrated style encompassing elements of both. We each need to find a personal style, one that is authentic and that works in our career. To do that, we need to understand the advantages and drawbacks of each approach as we form our own leadership style.

BRAINSTORMER

Define Your Leadership Style

Think of more typically female leadership traits: more collaborative, nurturing (like a coach or mentor), inclusive, less structured team-leader approach, intuitive. Think of more typically male leadership traits: more hierarchical with clearly defined roles, assertive, persuasive, rational, process oriented.

What kind of leader are you? Write down the adjectives that describe your leadership style.

Are you more in one camp than the other, or do you have a blending of traits?

Leadership Powwow

Unlike the masculine style of top-down leadership, female-style leadership encourages bottom-up and lateral input on leadership decisions and is even more apt to cede a certain degree of control to team members. In this sense, the female style of leadership is similar to the relatively new idea of "adaptive leadership" taught at Harvard's John F. Kennedy School of Government and other places.[4]

Rather than setting forth a strategy or vision for the company or team, the adaptive leader powwows with others to devise one together. Rather than being the chief problem solver, the adaptive leader creates a culture of problem solvers. The adaptive leader asks the tough questions and listens to other viewpoints, particularly those that challenge the traditional way of doing things.

The ability to work with others and consider alternative viewpoints is powerful. The reality is that working in silos doesn't produce the quantity or quality that results when people pull together as a team.

Likewise, a collaborative leadership style in which you share some control will get people to see you as a leader rather than a boss. A leader leads by listening and by inspiring hope and trust. A boss tells you what to do and you do it because it's part of a transaction, rather than for a loftier (read: better) relationship. In short, give orders and you're a boss. Share control and you're a leader.

A "Feeling" Leader

Our powers of empathy and our feeling approach can help us connect and engage with others as leaders. One of the key female-male differences that shows up on personality assessments like the *Myers-Briggs Type Indicator*® (MBTI®) instrument is between Thinking and Feeling preferences in making decisions.

On the one hand, people who prefer Thinking make decisions in a rational, logical, and objective way. They operate from a more detached viewpoint and like consistent rules with clear-cut causes and effects. Thinking types believe that emotion can distort decisions. If this sounds masculine to you, you're right. Around 60 percent of all men have a preference for Thinking in the Myers-Briggs assessment.[5]

Feeling types, on the other hand, live in the gray area. They see nuance in the world. They use empathy and emotional intelligence to supplement facts and provide meaning and solutions. They have a more subjective point of view and look at situations from the inside out—taking into consideration specific circumstances and the people involved. People who prefer Feeling seek solutions that bring about harmony and consensus. They adapt to the specific situation, rather than relying on black-and-white rules. If this sounds like you, then the odds are that you are a woman. Three-fourths of women tested as Feelers in the Myers-Briggs assessment in a national study.[6]

* * *

The majority of men are Thinking types;
The majority of women are Feeling types.

* * *

The Top Job

The most obvious question is, "If women have such strong leadership traits, why isn't the business world a matriarchy?"

And it's far from that. Women hold less than 3 percent of the Fortune 1000 CEO jobs. And only 15.7 percent of Fortune 500 corporate officers are women. That is virtually the same number as twenty years ago. Even in female-dominated industries, organizations, and groups, a male leader is often perched at the top of the organizational chart—what social scientists have dubbed the "glass escalator" for men in female-dominated organizations.[7]

For the time being, at least in most companies and organizations of any size, the top job has "male brand" written all over it. When men and women view leaders as men or father figures, the preferred leadership personality is assertive, competitive, and directive—all culturally masculine. This leaves women in a double bind. We are not viewed as having what it takes to lead, yet if we display the same male leadership traits without tempering them with softer female behaviors, we are devalued.[8]

What's a woman to do? As female leadership expert Alice Eagly told me, the idea that you can just rely on your feminine wiles and leadership strengths undermines your success. "Many roles, particularly leadership roles, require taking charge, being decisive, and engaging in masculine behavior. Leaders generally benefit from both culturally male and female personality qualities. Women need to learn how to be assertive, persuasive, authoritative, and, if possible, charismatic—all culturally masculine. It's the blend, the splitting the difference, that you see in so many highly successful women."[9]

* * *

You can't be a "servant leader."

* * *

Besides, because women leaders at the highest levels are so rare, we women are under more scrutiny and our missteps are magnified. When women fail as leaders, it's often a failure of leadership style, not a failure of ability or experience. You have to come across as decisive and in control, with a strong people-orientation. You must resist putting yourself in a subordinate role, asking for permission, as some women leaders do. Having an inclusive style is a strength, but at the end of the day, you have to make the hard decisions and lead.

The next Brainstormer will get you looking at your leadership style and thinking about where you want to go.

BRAINSTORMER

Getting the Career Outcome You Want

Think in terms of the outcome you want and work backward.

What would make an employer double your salary? What would you need to have as part of your self-brand profile that you don't have now?

What needs to be changed about your leadership style?

Circle the culturally male attributes that you want to incorporate into your leadership style: assertive, persuasive, authoritative, charismatic.

The In-Group

Ever since women began to climb the management ladder, observers have asked, "Do they have what it takes to lead large organizations?" The answer isn't as simple as yes or no.

In business, as in life, what you can't see can hurt you. Something sociologists call "in-group–out-group bias" is also in play. Bias is a challenge we all face. Most of the current business leaders—who are picking the new leaders—are men. Like members of any group, most men feel most comfortable with people like themselves, the in-group. They may have negative stereotypes about women, the out-group, but not necessarily.

The good news is that in the past couple of decades we have made some progress in changing perceptions about women in some industries that used to be male preserves. Today, we do see more female-brand leaders in professions like advertising, publishing, media, cosmetics, fashion, education, and health care, and in nonprofit organizations.

The Best of Both Worlds

Both the male and female leadership styles can be highly effective. It isn't as if one works and the other doesn't. Or that one style is good and the other is bad. Both have advantages and drawbacks.

But the best leaders have an "androgynous" style that blends the best of both male and female leadership traits.[10] Aspects of the female leadership style are more in tune with today's global business world, where women's ability to lead and persuade diverse groups of people can be a real advantage.

Today's leaders must increasingly use inclusiveness and relationship building to accomplish goals, since team members on many complex or global projects won't report to them or their bosses. These are ad hoc teams with multiple reporting lines. Yet the person who leads the team still has to get the job done. As the lines of authority blur in today's modern companies and projects demand cooperative teamwork and things move so fast, our collaborative, relationship-building, and communication skills will be a tremendous advantage, particularly if we hone our persuasive abilities and decisiveness.[11]

After all, the job of leaders is to create hope and optimism in their followers, what social scientists call "relational authenticity." In other

words, it's not enough to communicate your values, lofty and well inten-
tioned though they may be. You can't be a good leader unless you have
followers who believe in you and your ideas, and that takes a blending
of what is best in both the female and male leadership styles: being
inclusive yet decisive, intuitive yet rational, nurturing yet assertive.

Define *Your* Goals

There is a powerful reason why we don't see more women at the top,
and it doesn't have anything to do with ability or leadership style. Many
women don't want the top job.

Attaining success at the top of a Fortune 100 company or any large
organization requires extreme dedication and sacrifice. Most CEOs of
large corporations work sixty to one hundred hours per week. They are
workaholics by most definitions of the word, and studies show that most
workaholics are indeed men.[12]

❋   ❋   ❋

Many men at the top are workaholics.
Fewer women are willing to be workaholics.

❋   ❋   ❋

Even though some research studies show that the majority of female
middle managers aspire to the top levels of their companies, successful
women often tell me, as one did recently, "Yes, I'm ambitious. But not
for the top job or even number two in my company. My family is important, too. It's like what Jackie Kennedy Onassis famously said, 'If you bun-
gle raising your children, I don't think whatever else you do well matters
very much.'"

So it's not just lack of role models, the female leadership style, or
the glass ceiling that's holding some women back. Some women don't
want the executive suite. They don't want to be superwomen who focus
single-mindedly on work, as many male leaders are willing to do. It's
life before work.

Careers can be more complicated for women. We have multiple
roles and, arguably, richer lives. Many women have children, aging parents, active community commitments, or just an interest in staying
healthy and sane. Many are not willing to make the sacrifices required

to succeed at the highest levels, with frequent travel and late hours. Nor should they have to.

Ambition

It's not that women aren't ambitious. Of course we are, but we are often ambitious in a different way. Many women want a rich life as well as a great career and therefore take a broader view. As "Marci," an executive vice president of a multinational company, told me, "I want to succeed in every sense: at my job, as a wife, as a mother, with my friends, for the causes I believe in. Success for me is joy in all these things." When I asked Marci if she wanted to be president of her company, though, she told me emphatically, "No, today I'm very challenged and excited by my work, but I also need some time for my family and my interests. I would lose that if I moved any higher in the organization. So I sort of hit the glass ceiling, only it's one that I created."

And Marci is not alone. As a rule, women have more expansive interests and a more organic approach to careers, while men are oriented more toward planning and goals.[13] Recent research shows that 60 percent of women cite a dual focus on careers *and* family, while only 20 percent of women define work as taking precedence, which is the typical male view.[14] (The other 20 percent of women are home centered.)

Options

When women have choices, most don't make the typical male choice, a hard-edged focus on career and money. Many choose what one female executive called the "scenic route," moving from demanding line jobs to staff positions with less burdensome workloads so that they can manage everything. And that may hurt our success and salaries, but it also allows us to concentrate on the things that are important to us. Today, savvy companies are offering opt-in/opt-out and flextime programs so that women can succeed in both spheres.

Some talented women are deciding to completely opt out, at least for a while, and others are choosing to work part-time so that they can care for children or elderly parents. When the term *opting out* first came on the scene after an article in the *New York Times* in 2003, it generated a lot of controversy because some women see it as a step backward.[15]

The topic creates a division almost along generational lines—with younger women in favor of "choice feminism," as it's been branded, and women of a certain age basically reciting the Betty Friedan playbook and warning that it won't be so easy to opt back in. But that remains to be seen. Brenda Barnes, who headed up a division at PepsiCo, traded a staff of thirty thousand for three kids. Yet she was able to stage a dramatic comeback and today is chairman and CEO of Sara Lee. (There are no rules.)

Having options is always good. Let's face it, some women find work overrated and caring for children more enjoyable. In one study conducted by two Princeton professors, 909 employed women were asked to rate their feelings during sixteen different daily activities. At the top of the list in enjoyment were intimate relations and socializing, but next to the very bottom, just above commuting, was working.[16]

Ladies' Preference

The search for meaning is a driving force for many people, particularly women. Women talk about intrinsic goals like making a difference, having an impact in their communities, or doing good in the world. We want jobs that jibe with our values. And this often separates us from men. A 2005 study involving five hundred dual-income families showed that the quest for meaning and job autonomy becomes more prominent as a woman's level of education increases.[17]

Contrary to what you might think, the closer our work comes to the male model in terms of extreme time demands and responsibility, the less satisfied we are. Indeed, there has been an exodus of women from extreme jobs in law, investment banking, and technology in which workaholic schedules are the norm. These women are looking for challenge, meaning, and a kinder, gentler world.

While it's correct to challenge stereotyping of individuals, it's foolish to deny gender preferences. One famous study involved 34,000 people on a kibbutz in Israel in the 1970s. The idea was to create a utopian community with no sex-role stereotyping. Every job on the kibbutz was equally divided between men and women.

But it didn't stay that way. Gradually the men and women chose the jobs they preferred: 70–80 percent of the women chose people-oriented jobs working with children or in education, while men chose more systems-oriented jobs in factories, farming, construction, and maintenance.[18] So much for utopia.

The preference and talent that so many women have for people-related work do not sit well with some women, since they think that pushes us into lower-paying jobs. But the higher you go in the business world, the more important people skills are in determining your success. You can't be CEO or president of a company of any size unless you get people to follow you by rallying your team and building relationships with key clients and managers.

Create Brand Engagement

As a woman who is aiming for success—however you define it—one of your goals should be to engage people. Just as marketers strive for brand engagement connecting people with their product at every touch point, you should engage people with your product—Brand You.

Create interaction by asking lots of questions and listening. In conversation with others, listen to their points of view and share yours. And realize that whatever you say carries extra weight if you're the boss and will likely be broadcast throughout the company.

Be smart and establish a mechanism for getting feedback. It can be a weekly or monthly lunch with revolving executives from all levels across the organization. Don't meet just with senior people; meet with the mavericks, the outliers, the visionaries, and the youth of your organization. Make sure you get out of your office, too, and learn from your people. Visit regional offices. Visit international offices. Meet with customers, the small ones and the large ones—it will help you build brand awareness and brand engagement, not to mention become more informed as a leader.

Always try to incorporate the grand gesture (*geste d'estime*) to make a point, such as taking a major bonus or salary cut yourself when you are cutting back during tough times. The opportunities are endless, and word of mouth will be enormous. Nothing builds a brand as quickly as the grand gesture.

Little gestures can be big brand builders, too, like handwriting a short, thoughtful thank-you note to an employee for a job well done. One executive I know keeps the notes she's received in a special pouch for a pick-me-up on those days that things aren't going so well.

COMPANY LEADER	UP-AND-COMER
Being in the limelight	Working behind the scenes
Representing company brand	Being Brand You
Strategy	Operations
Outward focus	Inward focus

Adapt Your Brand

As a self-brander these days, you have to be prepared for just about anything and be ready to get your brand back on track quickly if it derails. The gap between job levels is larger the higher you go. The very talents that made you a great company treasurer—such as a fanatical attention to detail—are not the qualities you need as company president. Leaders who micromanage can't lead.

Every level demands a different type of leadership and brand experience, and different smarts and focus. People at the top of an organization need a more outward and big-picture brand orientation. You're representing the company brand to the outside world, after all.

At the highest level, you need to focus on strategy and execution but not get mired in the details. You need to inspire and motivate yourself and your team to win.

You'll also need to recruit a strong team, not loyal yes-people who will make you feel safe. Doris Kearns Goodwin's book *Team of Rivals* is a great management primer on leadership and team building. Rather than paying back his chief rivals in the presidential campaign by banishing them to political Siberia as most politicians do, Abraham Lincoln gave his rivals cabinet posts! He formed a team of his former rivals—the best and the brightest politicians—who were willing to criticize him and help him lead during that troubled time in American history. Lincoln nurtured and empowered his cabinet members so that he could take advantage of their collective intelligence and experience, characteristics of the female-oriented leadership style. President Obama mimicked Lincoln's srategy when he appointed former foes to top jobs in his cabinet in 2009. And it can be a very smart leadership strategy.

Leaders deaf to criticism and surrounded by yes-men can be a recipe for disaster.

There is a strong consensus that diverse groups lead to better problem solving and decision making. One interesting study found that men surrounded by other men of similar status jockey for the alpha role and are more likely to make high-risk financial bets. Women are not affected by this type of peer pressure. Another study tested the saliva of male financial traders to track testosterone levels during the day. The study found that higher testosterone levels could lead men to take higher risks, even affecting their ability to make rational decisions.[19] So be the type of leader who encourages diversity of thought.

You could also consider working with a leadership coach. (Corporate icons and celebrity endorsers have a slew of coaches who help keep them at the top of their game on the public stage.) The best choice would be a mentor with no agenda other than your success. You'll also run across people who are on a similar journey—spiritual and emotional soul mates—people who can teach you things or give you the courage to step up and take a stretch assignment.

Check for Brand Fit

Opportunities generally look scary at first. That's why most people pass them by. Sometimes, somehow, in our gut, maybe, we feel opportunity when everyone says to beware. When you feel it's right, take the leap.

Research shows that women are less likely to succumb to the "vividness bias," selecting a job because of bragging rights, such as a prestigious firm's name or a stupendous salary. Instead, they are more likely to take a holistic approach, looking at issues such as collegiality, travel, and office location.[20]

It's wise to make sure the company brand and culture fit with your brand and your lifestyle needs. Some "opportunities" can be a wrong turn and hurt your brand if you don't figure out how to mesh with the two. Look at Katie Couric. She left her leadership post as the reigning star of morning talk shows to take on the role of first woman anchor of the network evening news. Evening news was traditionally the place for gravitas, so it seemed like a smart move, and Couric was brought in to lure women and young people to the evening news on CBS.

At the beginning, this career move tarnished Couric's image. new assignments didn't capitalize on what made her a runaway success—her engaging style (backed by her high-wattage smile) of interviewing and talking to people in a casual format. It would be difficult for anyone to bring in young viewers to watch the evening news given the rise of the Internet, with its instant news and pundits. Couric famously revived her brand again with her widely viewed interviews of Sarah Palin during the 2008 presidential campaign. Katie regained her status as a star brand.

There's no playbook that works for everyone. It's a dynamic world, and the career marketplace is never static. That's why it's important to stay tuned in to what's shaping your marketplace, and keep your eyes open. Maybe your career will be a straight trajectory upward, but maybe not. Maybe you'll want to take some detours along the way, or even opt out for a period.

The career strategies that worked in your twenties and thirties may work when in you're in your forties or fifties, but maybe they won't. Or maybe the geographic area or industry you've targeted for Brand You is not as relevant today and you have to find the new high-growth ecosystems looking for talent.

Or maybe you're interested in other things and want to relaunch your brand in a new direction. If you're thinking like a leadership brand, particularly a female leadership brand, you can deal with whatever comes your way.

MADE IN AMERICA

Muriel "Mickie" Siebert
founder, Muriel Siebert & Co., Inc.

Only in America could my story take place. When I came to New York, I had five hundred dollars and a very used Studebaker car. Today I have eighteen honorary doctorate degrees even though I never completed college, and I became the first woman to buy a seat on the New York Stock Exchange.

I have an affinity for numbers and analysis. I can look at a page of numbers and they light up and tell me a story. When I started out on Wall Street, there were no women there other than the secretaries. I started out as a trainee in research at an investment firm and had to change jobs twice because men were making considerably more, or almost twice as much as me. Not long afterward, a major financial institution called in a commission order. They said they made money on a report I wrote. I was not registered at that time but later obtained my license. Since the major financial institutions valued my research, that meant that I could make money, and it gave me faith in myself. Being able to make money was important to me because my father died without money. We had to move from a nice house to a one-bedroom apartment, and we needed my uncle's financial help to support us.

On the job, I had to be flexible and learn to speak two different languages. To fit in on the trading desk, where every third word was a four-letter word, I had to talk like the guys, but for my clients, institutional portfolio managers, I was the complete opposite: analytical, thoughtful, and proper.

As a woman then, there were no female role models, so I just blazed my own path. It may have taken longer to build my clients' trust, but being a woman also helped me because it was so unusual at that time—I was unique. Part of my career goal was "Where can I go where there is no unequal pay situation?" That's why I decided to buy a seat on the stock exchange and work for myself.

Besides making money, I wanted my career to be about "How can I use my talents and abilities, and make a difference?" In 1975, on the first day members of the New York Stock Exchange could discount commissions, Muriel Siebert & Co., Inc., opened as a discount brokerage firm and later became the only woman-owned NYSE brokerage firm with a national presence. In 1977, I was appointed the first woman superintendent of banks in New York State, a position I held for five years. While I served as superintendent of banks, my firm was in a blind trust.

Now I am developing and sponsoring financial literacy programs for youths and adults, not just on investing but on the basics, which include credit cards, checking accounts, and income tax returns. These subjects are usually not included in required courses in schools. I want people to understand the basics of personal financial literacy. Their paychecks will go further, and we may be able to prevent another subprime mess from developing.

A woman's leadership style tends to be much more collaborative. We like to get various inputs and sometimes hire prople who are opposites to "fill in the gaps." Men often want to hire people just like themselves. I believe it's important to think in terms of a diversity of thought. Do you have the right mix of personalities? Of creative people and detail people? Old and young?

Gina Testa
vice president, Xerox

8

BORN TO NETWORK

At its core, networking is about connecting with other people, and that's something women excel at. Connecting is in our DNA. Given that we have the social gene, it's surprising that many career women don't have a great network, while many men do. Women often have a tight group of women friends but lack the big network of casual business acquaintances that men specialize in, and that's something we need to think about changing if we want to create more success in our lives.

We women tend to favor deep relationships with a group of close friends, a preference evolutionary scientists trace to our roots taking care of the family and the home. We also see this preference in playground studies: Most girls tend to pair up and play one-on-one with a single playmate, while boys are more likely to play with a series of different mates and then go off and play with a larger group.[1] When girls are in their teens and hormones kick in, the preference for intimate relationships with a small group of friends accelerates. The urge to connect deeply is something that stays with us our entire lives. These close personal relationships are extremely fulfilling to women because the connection is strong, deep, and committed.

*   *   *

Women connect intensely *with* small *groups.*
Men connect superficially *with* large *groups.*

*   *   *

A small group of deep relationships provides a reliable source of support and advice. But in the wider world of careers and brand building, a small, though intensely committed, group is not as advantageous as a large network of contacts, even if they are superficial.

The Male Model

The male social model is very different.

Whether it comes from years of helping one another score in team sports or it's in the male DNA, guys understand the mutual advantage of helping one another out. Men may talk about the Giants and the Jets or the Red Sox and the Yankees, but then business and the arranging of favors often follow. Many men can know someone casually or hardly at all and think it's no big deal to call him to arrange an informational interview or pitch him for a specific job opportunity. They feel comfortable pitching a friend or the friend of a friend.

While women favored close relationships, from an evolutionary point of view, men's specialty was forming a large network of shallower relationships. These broad networks were vital for developing social systems and culture.[2] So while most studies view women as more social, men are social, too, just in a different way.

Men, on the whole, seem to lack the need for deep connection. Not that they don't connect deeply with a significant other or buddy. It's just that men more commonly connect in a way that's more superficial from a woman's point of view. In fact, many of us would hardly consider male connections to be "relationships" at all. But male networks are powerful because of their size and range and men's comfort with making and accepting professional contacts. It gives them a major advantage in marketing their brand in the world.

✸   ✸   ✸

Men run in packs.
Career women should, too.

✸   ✸   ✸

There's no reason we women can't expand our relationship model to connect with more people on a less personal and less intense level. And many successful women have. But we all need to do it if we want to compete at a higher level or open up more career options.

Obviously, if we can form deep relationships, building a network of shallower acquaintances should be like playing in the minor leagues. And it's a smart strategy because the reality is that you can't do much on your own or with only a few supporters. We need to employ our connecting strength in a different way so that we can achieve real networking, and we have to understand its value.

Join the Networking Economy

After all, networking involves an economy. It's a hidden economy, but a very powerful one. It's an "economy of favors."

Networking is a bit like a business transaction, a system of informal quid pro quo. The networking trade works like this: I do you a favor, and the unspoken understanding is that if there is an opportunity to repay it, you will. A networking economy works only if there's trade back and forth. Otherwise, everything will come to a halt. It's an economy that men know well and many women are just learning about.

Strong Network = Career Capital

We all like to believe that career success is based on merit, but that is only a starting point. The truth is that participating in the networking economy will make you richer in terms of options and opportunities and, most likely, financially, too. Your network is like the brand alliances marketers form. If you don't understand how it works and don't participate, you will lose out on the opportunities and knowledge that others—your competitors—have.

For some women, networking transactions seem like a big deal. We may be more reluctant to ask for something unless we know someone well. But the best networks feed on lots of superficial relationships, and most people are willing to help. It's often as simple as phrasing it in terms of a "favor." A Stanford professor found that when he asked people to fill out a questionnaire in Penn Station, 57 percent agreed, but when he prefaced the request with, "Can you do me a favor?" 84 percent agreed.[3]

Women have been saddled with the reputation of being self-centered and not very helpful to others, particularly to other women. But I think that is largely a thing of the past and has been greatly exaggerated. Of course, many of us have run across women with this affliction—the queen bee syndrome. These are women who made it and don't want other women to come close to their position on the totem pole. As Madeleine Albright said, "I think there is a special place in hell for women who don't help other women."[4] (And it's not one of the nicer places either!)

The exchange of favors is what psychologists call "reciprocal altruism." A reputation for helping others and doing favors is an asset that attracts others to you.

Favor givers are attracted to those who reciprocate and punish those who take a favor and don't reciprocate. Believe me, the word will get out on what kind of person you are!

So if you have a reputation for helping others with contacts and professional information, you will be more successful because people will want to help you, too. Some women at the top of the networking game tell me that they often have to explain the networking economy to the women they are helping. Otherwise, it doesn't occur to them to reciprocate.

Ask and Want Not

When I talk about the networking economy, women often ask me, "How do I ask?" "How do I approach people?" "What are the words I should say?" In my experience, men don't labor over this as much. Men are more comfortable tapping a superficial acquaintance for a favor without all the soul searching and self-doubt that women go through. Maybe one reason is that in traditional dating, men have more experience socially in asking and women don't. But we don't have to undergo shock therapy to get good at it.

Sometimes, it's as simple as asking for a favor. You say, "I'm wondering if you can help me," and then you make a specific request. But most of the time you will need more finesse, especially if you want to seek help for bigger things. After all, unless you know someone very well, you can't call up and ask, "Can you help me get a job at your company?" or "Would you be my mentor?" Or "Will you give me your business?" That's tantamount to asking, "Will you lend me one hundred dollars?"

A more natural approach is to ask, "Can I brainstorm with you for fifteen minutes over the phone about how to move from my entry-level job to the next level? I know that you transitioned into various jobs in your own career, and I'd love to hear more about it."

The secret is to ask a question, allow the other person to talk, and then follow up with another question. Most people love to talk about their careers and offer advice, as long as they feel you don't expect them to get you a job. But as the relationship develops, you might ask if you can approach them from time to time as a sounding board. Then presto, you've got a mentor. And chances are high that your mentor will introduce you to others who will be valuable in your career journey. Just make sure to figure out ways to reciprocate!

Episodic Networking Syndrome

A lot of women think of networking as an important job-search technique. And it is. So when their jobs look dicey, they start networking madly to find a new one. Once they do, they go on their merry way until the next job dislocation, when they start networking madly again. It's sort of like yo-yo dieting—lose weight, gain weight. About the second or third time you do this, your network starts feeling used, and you're up the creek. (I suspect we all know a lot of people with this syndrome.) In short, network before you need to.

Successful networkers take a long-term rather than a short-term view. Networking is about meeting and connecting with people, sure, but it also is about access—to leverage. It can be access to people: people on the inside of a company you want to join, people in power or with the capital to invest in your venture, people who know lots of people, people who are looking for the talent you offer, or people who have the talent you need for your team. It can also be access to information. The higher you go in your career, the more you will be expected to be at the forefront of new ideas, deals, alliances, and opportunities for your company. Networking can put you in touch with the latest ideas and trends in your industry. It can help you tap resources that will keep your company in the lead. This sort of information gives you enormous clout and leverage.

So don't think you're done when you have a great mentor. In reality, you need a broad network of contacts and alliances. And you don't build it by thinking of what they can do for you. You build a powerful network by thinking of what you can do for the people in it.

Networking PhD

One of the savviest women networkers I've ever known (and I've known a few) was Phyllis Cerf Wagner. When Phyllis joined the ad agency, I was working on the "I Love New York" advertising campaign. Things were in a bit of turmoil since Governor Hugh Carey, who had championed the campaign, was leaving office.

Phyllis was a highly visible fund-raiser (a form of networker) for former mayor Ed Koch, who was running for governor. But Koch didn't win. Mario Cuomo did. It was an upset victory, and I was worried that we might lose the account. A change in management always puts an ad agency in the danger zone.

Phyllis used a lot of female strategies in her business networking. She played "matchmaker," connecting people she thought could benefit from knowing each other; nurtured client relationships, sending handwritten notes and making frequent phone calls to check in on people; and gave little gifts, often insignificant in price but thoughtful, like a recipe, an article, or a book she thought the other person would be interested in. Phyllis's pièce de résistance was hostessing parties in her home, inviting business associates as well as politicians, authors, and media and entertainment people. They were something to behold!

Initially, Phyllis didn't have a network with the new governor or his team. Gradually but steadily, she developed relationships with all the different levels of the incoming New York State team. She even made introductions to celebrities and government leaders such as Frank Sinatra and Henry Kissinger, who appeared in our new commercials. So we held on to the account, and Phyllis taught me that you don't have to be born into a network. You can do it the old-fashioned way—earn it.

Five Networking Tips

Here are five tips I've developed from observing great networkers like Phyllis:

- **Make a human connection.** First, find an area of common interest and build a *human connection* with the other person. If you don't connect with the person, you haven't really made a new contact for your network. Otherwise, you're just collecting business cards to make a personal phone book of people you can cold-call later.
- **Get out of your comfort zone.** Most people know a lot of people just like themselves and ignore those who don't match their profile, even though it's more advantageous to meet people of different backgrounds and from different places. And don't be afraid to meet people more important than you are. Remember, it's lonely at the top.
- **Do something for them so that an alliance is formed.** So many times you'll meet someone interesting and even exchange business cards, but the relationship never goes anywhere after the first meet-

ing. You need to lock in the relationship. Follow up with an article, a book, an introduction, whatever might be useful for the other person's career, to see if the connection can become a permanent part of your network.

- **Act like a hostess.** It's not easy walking into a room full of strangers, but if you don't mingle, you will be wasting your time. Successful networkers take charge by acting like hostesses. Walk up to a group and introduce yourself and then, after a while, move on to another group. You can go with a friend, but make sure to break up and get around the room individually. You can always rejoin from time to time.

- **Find out the best way to stay in touch.** Some women feel that networking has to be done in person, and, of course, there is no substitute for a warm smile, a strong handshake, and an eye-to-eye connection. But with busy people, that will be difficult, so use other ways to keep in touch. Remember, everybody's different. Some people like to be contacted via e-mail, while others prefer the telephone.

Network Far and Wide

Today there are women's networking groups of all types. There are industry groups for women. Many companies are supporting internal women's groups and funding speakers, workshops, and events that promote more female leadership. While men network on the golf course, women are putting together nontraditional women's networking groups through book clubs, knitting clubs, manicure groups, you name it.

❋   ❋   ❋

All-female network = Weak network.

❋   ❋   ❋

Since there are more men in positions of power, you'll need to have a lot of men in your network, too. Explore industry and business networking groups, political clubs, and nonprofit groups so that you'll be able to meet interesting and established women and men.

Networking can happen anywhere. One colleague left her job after a long career as president of a major company. Not sure what she wanted to do next, she made an unusual bet with herself. She vowed to say yes to everything that came her way over the next six months. Someone asked her to go with a group of volunteers to cheer up women prisoners over the holidays. Now she really didn't want to go, but she kept her promise, said yes, and went anyway. On the bus to the prison, she began chatting with another volunteer. And that conversation and connection led to a whole new career teaching at a university. The next Brainstormer will help you expand your networking sources.

BRAINSTORMER

Expand Your Network

You can't improve your network unless you benchmark where you are and measure how well you're doing with enlarging your network portfolio. Write down your current networking activities and the groups you are planning to explore, and don't forget to set a timetable.

Industry Organizations
Current:

Groups to explore:

Women's Networking Groups
Current:

Groups to explore:

BRAINSTORMER

(continued)

Nonprofit Organizations

Current:

Groups to explore:

Other Networking Groups

Current:

Groups to explore:

There's also something about old school ties. School affiliation can be so valuable as a networking tool that it's worth considering the quality of the university's alumni networking program when you choose a school. How good is the alumni database? What kind of networking and job support are available to graduates? It's the same with many sororities. A professional friend, Jill, told me that every job throughout her career came from a contact through Chi Omega sorority, but not necessarily women in her chapter. Once a sorority sister, always a sorority sister!

No Network—No Security

Many networking groups have a structured format, so you'll get a lot of practice with your thirty-second elevator speech. Many of these groups have in-person meetings and active Internet communities where people can share resources, pass on job leads, and provide support. There are even facilitated groups that cater to CEOs, CMOs, and other corporate elite that enable you to meet with your peers in different industries and coach one another on problems and opportunities.

As you network and expand the circle of people you know, you'll want to make sure that you include a variety of types in your network. Here are four mainstays:

- **Life support.** This is a small group, the numbers you use most on your speed dial. These are people you know well and who truly care about you, such as close family members and friends, both male and female.
  How to use. Use them for emotional support and as sounding boards on office politics, problems, romance.
- **Mentors.** These are senior, well-respected, well-connected people, and the more of them you have in your brand network, the richer your brand will be. High-profile mentors are like celebrity endorsements. You'll find they have a halo effect on your brand. Target people you admire and try to expand this group over time.
  How to use. As a rule, don't ask for more than about an hour of their time every month or so, and don't overstay your welcome. Use them as your think tank for advice and counsel, but be sure not to bombard them with too many follow-up e-mails and updates.
- **Connectors.** These are social people who know a lot of people and help you leverage your reach. They could be people in powerful jobs or not-so-powerful mid-level jobs. Don't overlook people in service professions, like lawyers and accountants or even hairstylists and therapists, who know a lot of people and like to connect them.
  How to use. Use them for getting introductions to other people and leads in organizations you are targeting.
- **Weak links.** Both important people and not-so-important people may be weak links. They are weak because you don't know them

that well, and you don't need to. Most women need to spend the most time building this group. Aim to make it a very large and varied group.

How to use. Use them for specific requests, such as a referrals or information. Most jobs come through weak links, so they are very valuable.

It's a big world out there, and you can be a big part of it (with your network in tow).

NETWORK, NETWORK, NETWORK

Pamela Paton

senior vice president, State Street Corporation

"Don't think you have to stay at one company" is the advice I give to women just starting their careers, even though I stayed at the same firm for over twenty-five years. I think it's vital for young people to explore options, find out about companies, find out who you are. This exploring usually involves shopping around for good fits and opportunities. I was able to do that, luckily, at the same firm, State Street Corporation.

I grew up about one hour south of Boston in blue-collar Taunton, Massachusetts. Dad died when I was seven, and by the time I was sixteen, I was working. My Depression-era mom was always stressing the importance of working hard and becoming successful. I put myself through college and started working for a program run by a major medical center, but they lost their contract and I was in need of an opportunity—fast. Networking paid off, and I was offered a job at State Street in Boston.

Moving from Taunton to Boston was a big move for me, but success is all about big moves. And I was ready for it.

Your boss can be very important in your career, and my first boss at State Street was great. She was a mentor as well as a boss and encouraged me in my entry-level job to be patient. "Something good is coming, perfect for you." It did come, in the form of traveling the country selling a revolutionary new product. I often felt amazed that I was this junior person representing the company alone with this important new product. They had confidence in me because they could see I had confidence in myself. I loved selling, not for the thrill of having a conquest, as may motivate men, but because of more female traits like caring for clients and helping them be successful. I viewed it as win-win.

I wasn't always in a good situation, though. After one company move early on, my new boss seemed to have an agenda of making a lot of changes, and I thought those changes might not be good for me. I was careful to network within the company so that others knew I was talented. I was able to zigzag out of that department and get back on track.

My advice to young people is to find a mentor. Find multiple mentors who will give you strong, constructive criticism, key people both inside and outside the company, both in the area where you work and out of it. Try to find people that you look up to. I've had a few that were my boss. Some others I approached. I would tell them why I admired them or how I enjoyed working with them on a project. And I'd ask, "Could you give me an hour a month?"

I would also suggest that you must be willing to take risks. My turning points came from taking risks by moving around in the company. I looked for opportunities to learn new business areas and skills, and if something looked good, I threw my hat in the ring. I was also willing to make lateral moves that may not have seemed like advancing, but if I saw potential in another department, I was willing to leave my comfort zone and do something new. And I never regretted it. Sometimes the best way to get ahead is by making a sideways move.

Having a wide network inside and outside the company gives you power. Seeking out mentors gives you wisdom. Zigzagging can make you more valuable.

Change can be stressful, but not changing could put the brakes on your career, and that can be stressful, too.

My life has been a journey to broaden boundaries and incrementally widen my viewpoint. I looked for paths that would open up my world professionally and personally. My teenage daughter, on the other hand, feels unbounded—she has grown up in a more global, diverse world and feels she can do anything. She's my role model.

Melinda Wolfe
senior vice president,
American Express

9

A BRAND FOR ALL SEASONS

Attractive and slim, wearing a chic pink Chanel suit, "Ophelia" cut an elegant image when we met. It was quite a contrast from the phone conversation we'd had a week earlier, when Ophelia emotionally described being laid off.

Up until that day, Ophelia was headed straight up the career ladder. From a family of Chinese American professionals, she attended prestigious schools and started her career in finance after business school. Life was sweet for several years, until the subprime mortgage crisis hit; then Ophelia was out on the street.

The economy was in the doldrums with no end in sight, and the financial services industry was undergoing a major retrenchment, with thousands of talented people being laid off. Ophelia diligently sent out her résumé and got no bites—not even one. And to make matters worse, no one even bothered to return her phone calls.

Do What the Branders Do

Ophelia had a classic marketing problem. As good as her product (Ophelia) was, her current positioning was no longer in demand. She couldn't go to market until she relaunched her brand around a good idea that fit the current market.

But when I asked Ophelia what her dream job would be, I could not believe her reply. Her goal had almost no relationship to what she had been doing or what she was looking for now. Ophelia's dream was to work in the luxury goods industry. Her twist was that she wanted to help Western luxury goods manufacturers market to the new money elite in China.

It was an interesting idea, particularly from a brand strategy per-spective. The U.S. economy was bad, and the financial services sector was undergoing a wholesale restructuring. Tens of thousands of jobs related to real estate and financial services were vaporizing. But in China, the economy was stronger. Just like a marketer who looks over-seas for growth when the domestic market is bad or mature, Ophelia had a compelling rationale for repositioning her brand for a growth market. The next Brainstormer will help you figure out a new direc-tion for your brand.

Ophelia's first challenge was to develop a personal-brand strategy and marketing plan that would point her in the right direction. Our first problem was Ophelia's glaring lack of credentials. We had to do a brand makeover. After all, Ophelia had no business experience in Asia what-soever, nor had she lived there, but she did have an interest because of her Chinese heritage. And she had no experience with luxury goods other than as an avid shopper at Chanel and Prada.

Your Brand Is What You Make It

We came up with a novel solution that would give Ophelia something akin to experience and get her brand back in demand. The idea was to conduct a market research study to measure perceptions of U.S. and European luxury brands that Ophelia could represent in China. The study would cover all the companies on Ophelia's hot list of places to work—from Ralph Lauren to Prada to Burberry to Louis Vuitton.

❋　　❋　　❋

Brand makeover: Connect
the dots to a new Brand You.

❋　　❋　　❋

Then we drafted letters to these luxury goods manufacturers, telling them that Ophelia was off to conduct a study of the high-end and "afford-able" luxury market in China and was including their brands in her study. Ophelia offered to meet with them and share her findings after she completed the study. She even got some "financing" from a friend who was a successful entrepreneur, which covered the cost of the trip and the research in return for access to her findings.

BRAINSTORMER

Assess What's Currently Important to You

What were the most important things that happened to you over the past year? Write down whatever comes to mind first.

Memorable people you met:

New interests and ideas:

Important events and career experiences:

Recurring thoughts and daydreams:

Next, look at your calendar and use a different-color pen to write down additional thoughts.

Now, looking at the lists above, put together your personal top ten list and ask yourself: What is surprising? What new directions am I gravitating toward? How can I explore it further? What is the overall theme or message?

Ophelia got responses from twelve out of the first fifteen companies that received her letter—a truly astounding response rate. Rather than looking for a job, Ophelia was offering something of interest to her target companies. Her success was no doubt propelled by the feeding frenzy of Western firms tapping the newly affluent segment of the Chinese market. It was clearly the right thing at the right time.

Before Ophelia went to China, she called or e-mailed all the people she knew who had business contacts there and asked them to arrange meetings. Every time she met with someone, she tried to get two or three additional names of people to meet. She also pitched people she didn't know, telling them what she was doing and asking for a short meeting. Before she knew it, Ophelia had practically every breakfast, lunch, and dinner spoken for and an impressive roster of business contacts in China, including many in the budding luxury goods market.

The Chinese businesspeople Ophelia contacted were hungry to build contacts with the West, so they were receptive to her calls—a very different situation from what she'd faced just a few months earlier, when no one had returned her calls. Plus Ophelia was packaged perfectly for the part, with her sassy haircut and classy clothes, and her ability to bridge East and West based on her background, language ability, and heritage.

Ophelia's strategy worked. Doing the market research gave her credibility with her new brand positioning, and by the end of her month-long stay in Shanghai, she was an expert on the luxury goods market in China. She knew which brands had the greatest cachet, and which didn't. She knew who the likely buyers were, and how to woo them.

This may sound like maneuvering, probably because it is maneuvering. We're all trying to maneuver in our careers, but most of us do it in a haphazard way or rely on wishful thinking. It's smart to maneuver strategically so that you can meet the people you want to meet, even if your goal isn't as bold as Ophelia's.

Fluid Branding

Whether you're developing your overall brand strategy or specific marketing tactics, think of it as both an analytical and a creative process. You have to use the rational left side of your brain to look at yourself objectively as a "product" in a broad marketplace. But brand strategy also employs the creative right side of your brain. And when you tap into your right brain, you open the floodgates of creativity that will help you position your brand and take more chances.

* * *

Thought + spark = new Brand You

* * *

Marketers develop business plans for their brands, and you should do the same for Brand You but realize that plans are an organic thing. You can't plan everything. You'll change, industries will change, or the market will change, as Ophelia found out. You can't possibly predict all of it, and you'll have to make adjustments along the way. But you can't accomplish anything without some planning, so the next Brainstormer will help get you started.

As one female executive told me, "Some women are process oriented, so they want a checklist for success, but career success is not a defined process. There isn't a one-size-fits-all formula. I can't tell them, 'Spend this percentage of your time on this, and that percentage on that.' What I tell people who work with me is, 'Figure out the results you want, and then figure out the best way to get them. You've got to create your *own* brand and visibility track. What worked for me won't necessarily work for you.' Part of my self-brand strategy is to find a 'mess,' something that isn't working, and offer to take on the assignment and fix it. Then I move on to a new mess."

Visibility Pays

You'll also want to gain visibility in some arena if you want to build a brand that's in demand. When something is visible and well known, we tend to think it is better than something that is not as well known. We attribute more positive traits to familiar things, and we're more likely to buy them even if we've only heard the names of the brands and know nothing more!

Women are notorious for being visibility challenged. Many women undervalue the importance of taking credit for accomplishments, volunteering to lead projects, or getting to know a range of senior executives.

Don't be afraid to toss your hat in the ring. Ask for assignments, and volunteer to lead or be a part of projects and new initiatives. When

BRAINSTORMER

Develop a Strategic and Tactical Marketing Plan

Develop a self-brand action plan to accomplish your goals over the next year:

Goals: Lay out two or three concrete goals for yourself.

SWOT: Recap the highlights of the SWOT analysis from chapter 2.

Target Markets: List the key people you intend to influence with your action plan.

Self-Brand Strategy: Define your brand positioning or big idea.

Tactics: Outline a series of specific marketing and professional activities that will help you reach your goals.

Time Frame and Measurement: Set concrete dates for the goals and individual tactics to measure success.

"Bria" was a beginning employee, she was itching for a promotion. "I didn't have all that much to do at the time, and with little to do, I get bored and restless, so I asked around for more work. One Friday, a helpful executive dropped a pile of reports on my desk and said, 'Why don't you write a summary of these?'"

Bria had a lost weekend, and the executive had a full report on Monday. He did it again, and she did it again. And before long, Bria was promoted to a bigger job. A little extra work can pay off a lot. So don't be afraid to ask.

When you're an important contributor or leader of a project or initiative, don't relinquish ownership, either—you can always share ownership. Remember the lesson of John Adams. Adams ceded the task of drafting the Declaration of Independence to Thomas Jefferson because he thought Jefferson was the better writer and regretted it for the rest of his life. "Jefferson ran away with the all the stage effect," he lamented, "and all the glory."[1]

Visibility means you're more likely to show up on Google when someone plugs in your name. Look at "Julia," who held a series of senior management positions in retailing. When a PR release about a new company initiative went out, Julia would tell the PR department to get a quote from one of her key lieutenants, not from her. Her recognition of subordinates made her a popular boss, but you can take it too far.

Now that Julia is in transition, she is virtually nonexistent on a Google search, and that's a problem. There's no paper or virtual trail to accentuate her impressive job history, so her role is diminished in the eyes of headhunters and prospective employers. Julia's competitors are other senior people with similar job histories who do have an impressive list of news clippings and links at Google, and that makes them more desirable.

Then there's "Kate," who worked at a pharmaceutical company for ten years but was not promoted to vice president, as were some of her colleagues who had similar responsibilities. Part of the feedback Kate received from her boss was that she lacked "visibility" in the company. Kate was so focused on the job and leading her team that she was virtually unknown at the senior levels of her company. Maybe her boss had recommended her for a promotion, but when the committee reviewed her nomination, Kate's name drew a blank. She was the invisible woman.

So how do you change that? After all, you can't run an ad with your picture in it at the company Web site.

Kate did several things. Since she had a large number of direct reports, she started a monthly brown-bag lunch and invited members of senior management to speak to her group about their areas or a company initiative. The lunches gave Kate a reason to call and get acquainted with senior managers she didn't know, and she followed up with them afterward to develop ongoing relationships.

Kate also volunteered to be a part of cross-functional teams that worked on key initiatives. This put her in contact with colleagues outside her comfort zone. And Kate worked on her speaking and presenting skills with a coach and with Toastmasters, so that she would feel more confident on the meeting stage.

The other thing Kate did was to ask her boss for a promotion, something she had never done before. (Remember, be a woman who asks!) Kate had been waiting for him to tap her on the shoulder and bestow the VP crown on her. Instead, she took the initiative and raised the issue herself.

Visibility Track

Visibility building can be viewed as a ladder—each level gives you more leverage. The first step may be as simple as getting out of your office. As "Jennifer," a senior exec at a technology company told me, "One of my missions is to encourage women to build visibility in our company. I tell them, 'Get out of your cubicle. Pick up your laptop and spend some time working in the lounge so you can meet people in other areas.'"

We often meet new people and form the ties that bind at these impromptu meetings. You find out what's going on at your company. You learn about shifts in power. You learn about new initiatives in which you can play a role. When you're seen, you're a contender.

If you are an employee, you can use nonprofit activities for building higher-octane visibility. Offer to chair a fund-raising drive, join a nonprofit board, or chair a committee. Many of these activities are covered in the local press, plus you will meet other interesting and successful people.

Nothing gives you more prestige and visibility than being on the board of a recognized corporation or nonprofit, since most boards are still an elite boys' club. Just as women are poorly represented at the highest levels of American business, women held 14.8 percent of Fortune 500 board seats in 2007.[2] A board seat gives you visibility and top-notch contacts as it broadens your experience. It will give your career a big boost, so seek it out when you're moving up the ranks. As one female board member told me, "Men seek out board seats at the height of their careers. Most women seek out board seats after they've retired. So they don't get the bang it could give their career."

Visibility is especially important when you're in transition or if you decide to opt out while raising your children. Many moms have impressive academic and career credentials, and being a mother gives you a certain amount of management cred, too. As Madeleine Kunin, the first and only woman governor of Vermont, said, if you've organized a birthday party for a five-year-old, you can run a political campaign! But it's even smarter to keep some visibility in the business world by taking on consulting projects or even forming mommy SWAT (Smart Women with Available Time) teams.[3] These all-mom teams are put together through temp agencies or, even better, by the moms themselves, to tackle business projects, usually on short notice with drop-dead deadlines.

Self-Promotion

"I don't buy into the adage that "all publicity is good publicity." As a self-brander, you want your brand-building and visibility tactics to lead to positive impressions about you. As in the world of branding, nothing is as powerful as word of mouth, and it's free! And good buzz generates more good buzz because we are all influenced by what others think.

Recently, more than 14,000 people were asked to rate new songs. One group was shown just the titles and the musical groups and asked to rate the songs. Then a second group was asked to rate the songs but was allowed to see how many times each song had been downloaded by the first group.[4]

Surprise! The opinions of the first group had a profound influence on how the second group rated the songs. The second group gave higher ratings to the songs the first group had liked, creating a snowball effect around the top picks. Positive word of mouth influences us all. It's as if a lightbulb goes on in our heads—"Gee, if other people say such wonderful things about her, she must be good."

It may be difficult to get on *Meet the Press,* but most of us can learn how to work the virtual room. And it's a valuable talent to cultivate, since Internet resources like blogs, Web sites, social networks, and e-zines are incredibly efficient for building visibility. And with today's hectic lifestyle, in which time is limited, leveraging the power of the Internet to build visibility and connections is smart.

If you work for a company, though, make sure you're in compliance with the company philosophy. Some companies encourage citizen bloggers as long as they don't post anything proprietary or damaging to the company. If you're an entrepreneur, however, visibility should be part of your lifeblood, and the Internet should be a core part of your visibility strategy because it's a low-cost way to promote yourself.

Public relations, whether digital or the old-fashioned media kind, is largely an ecosystem that works on relationships. Pitching a great story or sharing fresh insights on your blog is important, of course, but relationships make it much more likely that others will notice your pitch and put it on their media outlets or be receptive to mutual links.

Success comes to those who build a community around a distinct niche. In order to enter the media space effectively and build an audience, you need to check for room in the channel. Find a different spin, different content, a different attitude, a different something. For your PR efforts to be successful, whether through traditional media or new media, the "news" and the views it creates must not seem self-serving, nor must you appear to be keen on self-promotion. It pays to have a camera-ready sound bite when you're interviewed, but you must not come across like a person who's panting for publicity. As the saying goes, "If you drool, you lose."

Tend Your Reputation

Contrary to what we might think, people remember the bad over the good. Perceiving a bad event lights up the brain rapidly in MRI scans.[5] That's why we can remember vividly where we were when very bad events like the 9/11 terrorist attacks occurred but not much about what we were up to when a happy event occurred.

That's why good reputations take a long time to build but a short time to destroy. You have to *build* a reputation by racking up a lot of achievements and positive perceptions over time, but a high-profile fall from grace can blow all that good work to smithereens.

And to make things worse, bad reputations not only spread quickly and erase years of good deeds but are hard to shake. Bad reputations are sticky. That's why brand managers guard a brand's reputation and move quickly to remedy a problem before it gains currency.

* * *

Negative reputations are hard to peel off.

* * *

Not that you can't rebuild a brand after a fall. You can, but it isn't so easy, and sometimes the damage is permanent unless you can present a good redemption story. Look at public figures who got caught up in scandals. Martha Stewart spent some time in prison but was able to relaunch her brand, and today she's back at the top of her game, as strong as ever. Perhaps her "crime" didn't seem so bad in the scheme of things. Plus there is the sense that she came through the experience stronger and more human. Remember, Americans love redemption stories!

Pricing Power

The strongest brands have pricing power. You want to have pricing power, too, or people will think you are Brand X.

When something is more expensive, we think it's better than something that's cheaper. This may or may not be true in reality. Look at this wine taste test in which volunteers were asked to evaluate five wines. Each bottle was labeled by price: $5, $10, $35, $45, and $90 a bottle.[6] Naturally, everyone liked the most expensive wines best. Even the brains of the taste testers noticed the difference! Brain scans done as the tasters sipped and rated the wines showed that the expensive wines generated more activity in the area of the brain that responds to pleasurable experiences.

In reality, the wine labels were deceptive. The same expensive wine was in the $90 and the $10 bottle, and the $5 wine also was in the bottle labeled $45. But although these wines were the same, the brains of the testers registered less pleasure when they thought they were drinking a cheaper wine!

High price gives people an image boost, too. You will be assumed to be better than someone who is paid less.

Being paid well and feeling worth it professionally are relatively new for women. And the salary gap is changing for younger women, particularly in large cities.[7] The old gender gap was the pay gap. In 2007, women's pay, on average, was 80 percent of men's pay. But the gap is narrowing for women in their twenties. Census data from 2000 through 2005 show that women in their twenties made 89 percent of what men were paid. Amazingly, in big cities like New York, Dallas, Los Angeles, and Chicago, twenty-something women are making more—up to 20 percent more—than men.

Don't Give Up

What's the difference between those who go on to become brands and do great things, and those who don't? Mom called it the two Ds, drive and determination, traits she felt were key to success. Psychologists call it "self-efficacy"—a powerful belief in yourself, no matter what. Self-efficacy is different from self-esteem, which is an overall feeling of self-worth.

Self-efficacy is the unshakable belief that you've got what it takes and will succeed if only you persist.[8] It's keeping the faith until you figure out how to retool your brand and get traction with your target audience. It's telling yourself positive messages and not magnifying negative ones. (The brain builds new synaptic connections if the process is repeated enough.) It's not letting setbacks defeat you.

Remember, smart brands don't give up. They retool the brand and relaunch.

Brands typically go through a cycle that looks like a bell curve. The breakout period of high growth and visibility is followed by a mature phase and then a gradual decline. As you can imagine, it's one thing to get plum opportunities and visibility when you're young, new, and different, and quite another to get them when you're mature and no longer fresh and exciting. But masters of brand durability find ways to stay relevant and visible long after most brands fade from view. You can, too.

Remember, all brands—both people and commercial products—go through periods of struggle, sometimes very long periods of struggle. Take solace in the company you have during the tough times (and the great stories you'll be able to tell about your struggles and comeback). In Julie Andrews's new autobiography, *Home*, she recounts a screen test she did for MGM when she was twelve years old. "They needed to gussy me up a bit because I was so exceedingly plain," she revealed. With a hairstyle of ringlets mimicking Shirley Temple's, she took the screen test, only to be told, "She's not photogenic enough for film."[9] If J. K. Rowling had given up after her twelfth rejection, people would be saying, "Harry who?" Rowling ditched her first name, Joanne, and rebranded herself as J. K. since the publisher felt that a book aimed at boys but written by a woman wouldn't sell as well.

So if you feel like you're in a maze with no good place to go, keep forging on until you find the right opening. After all, it's the journey rather than the arrival that brings the greatest satisfaction. It's like the experiment with the monkey and the grape. The monkey feels the greatest reward not when he eats the grape but when he is sure that it's in his possession. And if things aren't working out, you can always rebrand yourself for a second act.

A Woman's Brand

The notions of self-creation and remaking one's brand are very American notions, practically a founding principle of this country. And there are second and third acts in American life. As one journey is ending, it is time to repositon yourself for the next phase, as Hillary Clinton did so well in her presidential bid concession speech in 2008.

Hillary Clinton's speech began, like the good ones do, with a bit of self-deprecation. "Well, this isn't exactly the party I'd planned, but I sure like the company." She went on to thank all the people who supported her, wrapping her thank-you in our most popular myth, the American dream: "the moms and dads who came to our events, who lifted their little girls and little boys on their shoulders and whispered in their ears, 'See, you can be anything you want to be.'"

Hillary told stories in sentences so well crafted that you felt you knew these people. She asked her followers "to take our energy, our passion, our strength and do all we can to help elect Barack Obama the next president of the United States." And she took a page from Obama's own playbook to say: "Yes, we can!" She capped off her description of the work that remains with a rallying refrain repeated in commanding cadences: "That's why we need to help elect Barack Obama our president." She seemed so ready to help Obama that she might even be willing to answer the phone at 3 A.M. for him.

Hillary reached out to women, young and old, many of whom had tears in their eyes, and reminded them of what had been accomplished. "Could a woman really serve as commander in chief? Well, I think we answered that one." And later in the speech, in a memorable visual metaphor, "Although we weren't able to shatter that highest, hardest glass ceiling this time, thanks to you, it's got about 18 million cracks in it. And the light is shining through like never before, filling us all with the hope and the sure knowledge that the path will be a little easier next time." Hillary saluted the suffragists at Seneca Falls in 1848 and all the women who fought for women's and civil rights, leading to the refrain, "because of them . . . , because of them. . . ."

The speech was as much about Hillary and her women legions as it was about Obama, but she did give an acceptable amount of praise considering how new it was for her to be an Obama supporter. It was a speech big in scope, graceful in wording, inspiring in vision—the speech of a statesperson, not a politician. Later, Clinton was given the chance to show her statesmanship, when she was appointed Secretary of State in 2009.

A Brand for All Ages

There are no hard-and-fast rules for successful branding or successful leadership for women. You'll have to use your own brain and instincts, your female-based aptitudes, and your special uniqueness and abilities—that's what makes it fun and interesting. But here are some guidelines to keep in mind as you take your female brand out into the world:

- Sunny beats gloomy.
- Sparkle beats drabness.
- Authenticity beats pretending.
- Consistency beats muddled.
- Difference beats conformity.

- Strategy beats luck.
- Tactics beat inaction.
- Engagement beats aloofness.
- Visibility beats a low profile.
- Perception beats reality.

Just as no two people are the same, even if they are twins, no two people have the same brand assets. As a self-brander, your job is to manage the asset that is you through the good times and the bad.

The good news is you are in charge of your brand—in crafting your brand and taking it out into the world. You are the brand manager and the creative director. You are the screenwriter and the editor. You get to select the core brand concept, your message, and the direction (including changes in direction) for your brand. (The bad news is also all of the above.)

Tap into your powerful woman's intuition and instincts to help you zero in on new ways to keep your brand in demand.

Create the brand that is right for you and the action plan that takes you in the direction you want in your career as well as in your life, that complements your motivations and aspirations, that takes advantage of your female mindset and your personal inclinations. When your brand is focused, relevant, and engaging, people will take an interest in your success. You will be maximizing your most important asset—you.

A WOMAN'S PLACE IS IN THE HOUSE (OF REPRESENTATIVES)

Kirsten Gillibrand

U.S. Senate, New York

Being elected to the United States House of Representatives and later being appointed to the U.S. senate have been unparalleled honors. I had long dreamed of doing public service, but to represent our New York families in Congress has been more exciting and more rewarding than I could have ever imagined.

My story began long before I was born, with a family of strong accomplished women who would be my inspiration. Many today still think of women in government as unusual, but in my grandmother's time it was virtually unheard of. In a time when the ink was barely dry on the Nineteenth Amendment giving women the right to vote, my grandmother was involved in politics and advocated that women's voices be heard.

Starting in the late 1930s, my grandmother Dorothea "Polly" McLean Noonan was a secretary in the New York State Legislature in Albany. At the time, all the secretaries were women and nearly all of the legislators were men. My grandmother wanted to be involved not only in legislation and government but in the politics of the day.

She believed women should have a stronger voice in who represented them and their families, so she began to organize at the grassroots level. She helped lead the effort to organize the women of the legislature and then broadened the network of women to form the first Women's Democratic Club in the county of Albany.

My grandmother taught me the importance of broad-based activism. I watched her engage women at every level of the political process, from going door-to-door, staffing phone banks, and stuffing envelopes to encouraging them to be stronger advocates. Because of her commitment and leadership, women's voices were heard, and they made a difference in the agenda of the day.

One of the greatest gifts my grandmother gave me was simply taking me with her. I remember many fall afternoons as a young girl passing out flyers, putting bumper stickers on cars, and sitting in campaign headquarters stuffing envelopes in the company of many fascinating women.

I had another strong role model—my mother, Polly Noonan Rutnik. She also was a trailblazer and set out to make a difference as a lawyer when few women chose such a profession. She was one of only three women in her law school class, and her experiences were pretty shocking. She had a criminal law exam scheduled for the day she went into labor with my older brother. Being progressive, her law professor was gracious enough to let her take the exam the next day!

As an attorney, my mom became an advocate for families adopting children, buying their first homes, and drawing up wills. I became a lawyer because I wanted to learn how to be the strongest and most effective advocate I could be.

As a young lawyer, I soon became interested in getting involved politically. I followed in my grandmother's footsteps and began to organize women. I became involved in the Women's Leadership Forum, a national organization founded to engage women in presidential politics. There were very few women under the age of forty involved, so I set out to change that. I founded a local Women's Leadership Forum network. We taught younger women how to organize, raise money, and be more effective issues advocates. I began to think about doing public service full-time but did not really know how to make that transition.

One day, I was at a Women's Leadership Forum event and Andrew Cuomo, secretary of the Department of Housing and Urban Development (HUD), was giving a speech about the importance of public service. After his talk, I approached him, introduced myself, and told him about my interest in serving, and he asked me to come to Washington to interview for a position as special counsel. After the interview, Mr. Cuomo offered me the job, and I accepted.

As special counsel at HUD, I was able to work on legislation that I thought mattered—such as the New Markets Initiative, intended to invest public and private money in low-income areas to build infrastructure and affordable homes. But mostly, it solidified my interest in doing public service full-time. Over the next few years, I thought about where I could best serve and decided that my training would lend itself best to serving at the federal level as a member of Congress.

In the meantime, my husband and I decided to raise our family where I had grown up, near my parents, brother's family, aunts, uncles, and cousins, in upstate New York. Once upstate, we decided that it was time to try to make that shift to full-time public service. I ran for the U.S. Congress representing the 20th District of New York.

I was privileged to win the seat and the greatest honor to represent more than 600,000 upstate New Yorkers in Washington. In 2009, I was appointed by Governor Paterson to fill the U.S. Senate seat formerly held by Hillary Clinton. I stay in touch with my constituents by holding town hall "Congress on your Corner" meetings at grocery stores, coffee shops, bookstores, and community centers, where I talk to folks about the issues that matter to them. I usually learn a tremendous amount and often get the best ideas for legislation directly from my constituents at these gatherings.

I hope to be a role model for young women, as my mother and grandmother were for me. I hope we will see more women in local and national office because they can see it is possible. I know my grandmother would be proud of me and of all the women who work every day to provide for their families and make a difference in their own special way.

THE FINAL WORD

It's Up to You

Gender difference mirrors fundamental concepts of reality: negative and positive, matter and void, yin and yang, male and female. We're each a product of many things—our time, our place, our family—but nothing is as fundamental to our identity as our gender.

After centuries of a profound anti-female bias, we have finally achieved an enlightenment of sorts. And one of the most positive developments for the world's future is the celebration of the female mindset. I have attempted here to give a practical guide on how women can achieve career and life success by taking advantage of female strengths and further transform the workplace with the female brand.

With our collaborative, inclusive leadership style, we're leading in a way that doesn't seek to have power over people as much as to empower people. Women are opening up the forum for broader communication and problem solving in the professional world, a distinct advantage in today's competitive, global workplace. We have powers of empathy and intuition that help us read a room or situation, or gauge how we're coming across. Women aren't afraid to put caring and warmth into the professional equation, to create a personal feeling as leaders. After all, it's in our DNA to cultivate connection and relationships. Many of us use our verbal agility to shine in communicating at work and our edge in visual identity to bring color and style to the workplace.

Branding gives you a process for maximizing these female-based assets and the unique asset that is you. Self-branding gives you the tools to fill in the missing pieces of the puzzle so that others will have positive impressions about Brand You.

There are so many ways that we as women can define and build success for ourselves. In the past, success was often one-dimensional, defined in terms of workplace success. Women want that, too, but have many other realms where we define our success. And we are helping to transform the work world in important ways. Today, the workplace is becoming more humane, with more collaboration and more discussion of issues.

At every point in your professional life, there are different options and opportunities. But if you're true to yourself and take charge of your brand, you'll find the right strategy and tactics to withstand any storm and address the big issues in your life.

As Mom said, "It's up to you."

BRAINSTORMERS

ACKNOWLEDGMENTS

Female intuition gave me the idea to write this book, but acting on it took the inspiration, stories, suggestions and support of hundreds of people.

First, my special thanks to Gary Andrew Gulkis, my book collaborator who provided the poet's gift for language to know the right word and to help me craft the text with style and elegance. As a representative of that other gender, he provided invaluable balance, insight and humor and helped to keep me challenged and focused on the larger truth. This book became dramatically better through his generous participation.

In developing this book, I interviewed well over 100 women, successful women one and all – women in their 20s, 30s, 40s, 50s, 60s, 70s. What a treasure trove of insights and passion about women and success. Thanks especially to the women who let me use their stories and point of view in my book: Meenu Chhabra, Deborah Elam, Paula Forman, Kirsten Gillibrand, Joi Gordon, Elizabeth Hitchcock, Rosalind Hudnell, Fiona Hutchinson, Graciela Meibar, Pam Paton, Barbara Res, Marcia Roosevelt, Carol Ross, Edwina Sandys, Muriel Siebert, Gena Testar, Billie Ida Williamson, and Melinda Wolfe. I want to thank professors Alice Eagly, Roy Baumeister, and David Klappholz for their insight.

The list of people I interviewed is too long to detail here, but I especially want to thank the following for their suggestions, stories and thoughts on the female brand: Sylvia Acevedo, Yoshiko Aiba, Jean Andersen, Iris Apfel, Nomi Bachar, Roy Baumeister, Aishwarya Bhat, Tom Blanco, Kevin Renee Bishop, Nora Brennan, Carolyn Buck Luce, Georgina Carnegie, Arlene Castrovinci, Jodi Charles, Sue Chiafullo, Karen Christensen, Kathy Connelly, Paul Copcutt, Tim Davis, Kathie DeChirico, Eli Dickson Vicki Donlon, Theresa M. Ellis, Anne Erni, Susan Esper, Tiffany Esposito, Dr. Vincent Esposito, Sandy Evans, Joe and Veronica Fabio, Joan Ford, Barbara Glasser, Sherry Glazer, Maria Gotsch, Susan Jacobs, Jeannie Kahwajy, Mary Kapka, Karen Kesner, Beth-Ellen Keyes, Jill Klein, Barbara Krafte, Pamela Larrick, Starlin Leitner, Roberta Maguire, Terry Mamendo, Pauline Mohr, Faith Monson, Diane Morgan, Elizabeth Nieto, Ginny O'Brien, Young-Mi Park, Vasso Petrou, Marcia Roosevelt, Nancy Rutter, Eileen Smith, Beverly Tarulli, Sherri Smith, Lisa Watts and Margaret Yelland.

Writing a book can be an arduous ordeal. That's why having a great publishing team is so critical, and my team at Davies-Black actually made it fun. (Well, almost). Top of my list to thank are Laura Lawson and Laura Simonds at Davies Black. Thanks also to the team who took my book through its final phases with grace and attention: Chuck Dresner, Erika Heilman, and Wendy Lazear. Special thanks to Laura Berkowitz Gilbert who designed the cover jacket and interior book graphics, and made the book look beautiful and strong just like the topic.

I want to thank my three sisters: Kevin, Jean, and Joan—my Sisterhood of Supporters. Many thanks especially to my husband, Mike, and my son, Ramsey, whose support and love were necessary for this author to write, and who had to patiently put up with me carrying my laptop everywhere we went. Thanks guys.

ABOUT THE AUTHOR

The belief that we can recreate ourselves to fit our dreams is a deeply American idea, one that Catherine Kaputa's own life reflects. Catherine began her career as a Japanese art historian at the Seattle Art Museum, and later worked on a Ph.D. at Harvard University. She experienced her first personal branding crisis when she decided that "Japanese art historian" wasn't her brand, even though she had invested two years studying in Japan at Tokyo University and had translated a book from Japanese.

Catherine came to New York to rebrand herself to work in marketing and communications—a difficult transition given the profound differences between the academic and commercial worlds. Persistence led her to branding pioneers Al Ries and Jack Trout at Trout & Ries Advertising, who decided to take a chance on her. Later, Catherine worked at Wells, Rich, Greene as the Management Supervisor on the I (Heart) New York account. She gained valuable experience supervising the TV commercials featuring Broadway musicals and celebrities, which received numerous creative awards.

Interested in expanding her portfolio of experience by working from the client's side, Catherine moved to Wall Street, where she was Senior Vice President, Director of Advertising and Community Affairs at Shearson Lehman Brothers and later Citi Smith Barney for more than ten years.

As Catherine was taking her son to preschool on September 11, 2001, the two towers of the World Trade Center fell down, four blocks from where she worked. She then decided to start her own business as a personal branding and career coach. She also began teaching at New York University's Stern School of Business.

Catherine decided to share the techniques she developed as a career consultant. The result was the book, *U R a Brand! How Smart People Brand Themselves for Business Success*, winner of the Ben Franklin award for best career book 2007 and a bronze IPPY award (www .urabrand.com).

Catherine developed speaking presentations for women's business organizations, she identified a need for more analysis of the unique career challenges women face in the workplace. In response, she wrote *The Female Brand: Using the Female Mindset to Succeed in Business* (www.femalebrand.com).

Catherine loves to hear from her clients and readers. She can be reached at www.selfbrand.com.

NOTES

Preface

1. This study discussed by Professor Donelson Forsyth was broadcast in *The Infinite Mind,* on National Public Radio. See "The Infinite Mind: Groups" at www.infinitemind.org or www.lemedia.com/mind9929.htm. An Israeli study with preschoolers showed that boys are fifty times more likely than girls to use competition and physical means, while girls use talking and taking turns. Susan Pinker, *The Sexual Paradox: Men, Women and the Real Gender Gap* (New York: Scribner, 2008), 199–200.

2. The fact that women are twice as likely as men to suffer from depression has been widely documented; see "New Report on Women and Depression: Latest Research Findings and Recommendations," American Psychological Association, www.apa.org/releases/depression report .html. More than 90 percent of people with eating disorders are women; see www.4woman.gov/owh/pub/factsheets/eatingdis.htm. For information on male aggression, violence, and alcohol abuse, see *Alcohol Alert,* National Institute on Alcohol Abuse and Alcoholism, no. 38 (October 1997), http://pubs.niaaa.nih.gov/publications/ aa38.htm.

Introduction

1. Angela Braly, "Fortune 500 Women CEOs," http://money.cnn.com/ galleries/2008/fortune/0804/gallery.500_women_ceos.fortune/.

Chapter 1

1. See the Catalyst Web site, catalyst.org/pressroom/pressdoublebind.shtml; and Lisa Belkin, "The Feminine Critique," *New York Times,* November 1, 2007.

2. Many women I interviewed made this observation about Hillary Clinton's double bind because the 2008 Democratic presidential primary race was taking place. See also Carol Hymowitz, "Looking at Clinton, Seeing Themselves," *Wall Street Journal,* available at www.wsj.com.

3. Simon Baron-Cohen, *The Essential Difference, Male and Female Brains and the Truth About Autism* (New York: Basic Books, 2004). Baron-Cohen talks about this study at http://www.edge.org/3rd_culture/ baron-cohen05/baron-cohen05_index.html.

4. Susan Pinker, *The Sexual Paradox: Men, Women and the Real Gender Gap* (New York: Scribner, 2008).

5. Louann Brizendene, *The Female Brain* (New York: Random House, 2007).

6. B. A. Shaywitz et al., "Sex Differences in the Functional Organization of the Brain for Language," available at http://www.ncbi.nlm.nih.gov /pubmed/7854416; A. M. Galaburda, *Dyslexia and Development: Neurobiological Aspects of Extra-Ordinary Brains* (Cambridge, MA: Harvard University Press, 1993); K. R. Pugh et al., "Cerebral Organization of Component Process in Reading," *Brain* 119 (1996).

7. Kolata, "Man's World, Woman's World?"; This research was done by Dr. Sandra Witelson; see Susan Pinker, *The Sexual Paradox*, p. 46. Baron-Cohen, *The Essential Difference;* Cahill, "His Brain, Her Brain."

8. The fallacy of a larger brain equating with higher IQ in men was made and debunked again as recently as 2005; see http://education.guardian .co.uk/higher/news/story/0,,1635507,00.html.

9. University College London professor Adrian Furnham based his findings for the "male hubris, female humility effect" on thirty international studies of how men and women rate their own brainpower. Read *Newsweek*'s interview of Furnham at www.newsweek.com/id/101079.

10. See Diane F. Halpern, Camilla P. Benbow, David C. Geary, Ruben C. Gur, Janet Shibley Hyde, and Morton Anne Gernsbacher, "Sex, Math and Scientific Achievement," *Scientific American,* November 28, 2007.

11. Joshua Rosenbloom, an economist with the University of Kansas, conducted this study, which will be published in the *Journal of Economic Psychology*. The study is discussed by Elaine McArdle, in "The Freedom to Say 'No,'" *Boston Globe,* May 18, 2008.

12. For the SMPY study see www.vanderbilt.edu/Peabody/ SMPY/. See also McArdle, "The Freedom to Say 'No.'"

13. Pinker, *The Sexual Paradox;* Sara Rimer, "Math Skills Suffer in U.S., Study Finds," *The New York Times,* October 10, 2008.

14. Professor David Klappholz makes this argument for attracting women into IT: David Klappholz, "Recruiting Young Women Into and Retaining Them in Computing-Related Majors: An Initiative Based Upon 35 Years of Psychology Research." See http://membernet.acm.org/#Recruit.

15. Read Roy F. Baumeister's delightful "Is There Anything Good About Men?" address to the American Psychological Association, 2007, available at http://www.psy.fsu.edu/~baumeistertice/goodaboutmen.htm. I am also indebted to Professor Baumeister for sharing his views on

male–female differences and a range of gender topics in a phone conversation, in 2008. See also Roy F. Baumeister and Kristin L. Sommer, "What Do Men Want? Gender Differences and Two Spheres of Belongingness: Comment on Cross and Madson (1997)," *Psychological Bulletin* 122, no. 1 (1997): 38–44.

16. See William J. Sabol, Heather Couture, and Paige M. Harrison, "Prisoners in 2006," *Bureau of Justice Statistics Bulletin,* 6.

17. Baumeister, "Is There Anything Good About Men?"; Susan Pinker, *The Sexual Paradox.*

18. Susan Pinkjer, *The Sexual Paradox*; Alice H. Eagly and Linda L. Carli, *Through the Labyrinth: The Truth About How Women Become Leaders* (Boston: Harvard Business School Press, 2007); Dee Dee Myers, *Why Women Should Rule the World* (NY: Harper Luxe, 2008).

19. See Goleman, *Social Intelligence: The New Science of Human Relationships* (New York: Bantam, 2007).

Chapter 2

1. Dan Heath and Chip Heath, "Made to Stick," *Fast Company,* July/August 2008, 67.

2. See Scott Adams's blog, http://dilbertblog.typepad.com/ the_dilbert_blog/2007/07/career-advice.html.

3. See Stuart Adams, "Leading CEOs: A Statistical Snapshot of S&P 500 Leaders," January 2008, www.spencerstuart.com/research/articles/975/.

4. See *Forbes Life/Executive Woman,* April 2008, 18.

5. *Forbes,* April 21, 2008, 21.

Chapter 3

1. "Women Like Women More Than Men Like Men, According to Study," *Science Daily,* December 22, 2004. For an account of research done by Purdue's Women Studies Program, see *Journal of Personality and Social Psychology,* October 2004.

2. Roy Baumeister, "Is There Anything Good About Men?" address to the American Psychological Association, 2007, available at http://www.psy.fsu.edu/~baumeistertice/goodaboutmen.htm; Alice H. Eagly and Linda L. Carli, *Through the Labyrinth: The Truth About How Women Become Leaders* (Boston: Harvard Business School Press, 2007).

3. The Q Score was developed in 1963 by Marketing Evaluations, Inc., a U.S. company based in Manhasset, New York, to measure the familiarity and appeal of a brand, company, celebrity, cartoon character, or television show.

4. Stephanie Rosenbloom, "Googling Me and Finding You: Names That Match Form a Bond," *New York Times,* April 10, 2008, A1, A22.

5. Giacomo Rizzolatti and Corrado Sinigaglia, *Mirrors in the Brain: How Our Minds Share Actions and Emotions,* trans. Frances Anderson (Oxford: Oxford University Press, 2008); Marco Iacoboni, *Mirroring People: The New Science of How We Connect with Others* (New York: Farrar, Straus and Giroux, 2008).

6. Simon Baron-Cohen and Claudia Strauss, "Is Empathy Gendered, and If So, Why? An Approach for Feminist Psychological Anthropology," *Ethos* 32, no. 4 (December 2004): 432–57; Simon Baron-Cohen and Sally Wheelwright, "The Empathy Quotient: An Investigation of Adults with Asperger Syndrome or High-Functioning Autism, and Normal Sex Differences," *Journal of Autism and Developmental Disorders* 34, no. 2 (2004): 163–75; Susan Pinker, *The Sexual Paradox: Men, Women and the Real Gender Gap* (New York: Scribner, 2008).

7. Geoffrey B. C. Hall, Sandra Witelson, F. Henry Szechtman, and Claudia Nhmias, "Sex Differences in Functional Activation Patterns Revealed by Increased Emotion Processing Demands," *Neuroreport* 15 (2004): 212–23; Turhan Canli et al., "Sex Differences in the Neural Basis of Emotional Memories," available at http://www.pnas.org/content/99/16/10789.abstract.

8. See Baron-Cohen, *The Essential Difference.*

9. Mirror neurons were discovered by Giacomo Rizzolatti. See Rizzolatti and Sinigaglia, *Mirrors in the Brain;* and Iacobono, *Mirroring People.* The DNA prediction was made by V. S. Ramachandran, a neuroscientist at the University of California, San Diego. See also Christopher F. Chabris, "The Reflection Reflex: How Brain Researchers Pinpointed the Inextricable Link Between Seeing and Doing," *Wall Street Journal,* May 31–June 1, 2008.

10. Baron-Cohen, *The Essential Difference;* Daniel Goleman, *Social Intelligence: The New Science of Human Relationships* (New York: Bantam, 2007); Robert Lee Hotz, "How Your Brain Allows You to Walk in Another's Shoes," *Wall Street Journal,* August 17, 2007, http://online.wsj.com/article/SB118728841048999914.html.

11. Jeff Goldberg, "My Amygdala, My Self," *The Atlantic,* July–August 2008.

12. For examples, see Gerd Gigerenzer, *Gut Feelings: The Intelligence of the Unconscious* (New York: Viking, 2007); Malcolm Gladwell,

Blink: The Power of Thinking Without Thinking (Boston: Back Bay, 2007).

13. Jared Sandberg, "Dreaming About Work Can Be a Nightmare, but It Beats Insomnia," *Wall Street Journal*, January 15, 2008.

14. David Van Biema, "Neuroscience: My Nose, My Brain, My Faith," *Time*, January 23, 2008, 47.

15. Baron-Cohen, *The Essential Difference*.

16. Ibid.

17. Goleman, *Social Intelligence*.

18. Ibid.; Benedict Carey, "You Remind Me of Me," *New York Times*, February 12, 2008.

19. This research was cited in Goleman, *Social Intelligence*, 275; for the full study, see Michael T. Newcommbe and Neal M. Ashkanasy, "The Code of Affect and Affective Congruence in Perceptions of Leaders: An Experimental Study," *Leadership Quarterly* 13 (2002): 601–4.

20. Shankar Vedantam, "Salary, Gender and the Social Cost of Haggling," *Washington Post*, July 30, 2007, A7.

Chapter 4

1. Amanda Lenhart, Mary Madden, Alexandra Rankin MacGill, Aaron Smith, "Reports: Family, Friends, and Community," December 19, 2007, http://www.pewinternet.org/PPF/r/230/report_display.asp.

2. "Digital Natives: Teenage Girls as the Cyberpioneers of the Internet," Berkman Center for Internet & Society, Harvard University, http://cyber.law.harvard.edu/node/3941.

3. Diane F. Halpern, Camilla P. Benbow, David C. Geary, Ruben C. Gur, Janet Shibley Hyde, and Morton Anne Gernsbacher, "Sex, Math and Scientific Achievement," *Scientific American*, November 28, 2007; Simon Baron-Cohen, *The Essential Difference: Male and Female Brains and the Truth About Autism* (New York: Basic Books, 2004); Louann Brizendene, *The Female Brain* (New York: Random House, 2007); Larry Cahill, "His Brain, Her Brain," *Scientific American*, April 25, 2005; Gina Kolata, "Man's World, Woman's World? Brain Studies Point to Differences," *New York Times*, February 28, 1995.

4. Bennett A. Shaywitz et al., "Sex Differences in the Functional Organization of the Brain for Language," available at http://www.haskins.yale .edu/Reprints/HL0954.pdf; A. M. Galaburda, *Dyslexia and Development: Neurobiological Aspects of Extra-Ordinary Brains* (Cambridge,

MA: Harvard University Press, 1993); K. R. Pugh et al., "Cerebral Organization of Component Process in Reading," *Brain* 119 (1996).

5. Baron-Cohen, *The Essential Difference;* Susan Pinker, *The Sexual Paradox: Men, Women and the Real Gender Gap* (New York: Scribner, 2008); Brizendene, *The Female Brain;* Cahill, "His Brain, Her Brain"; Kolata, "Man's World, Woman's World?"; Halpern, Benbow, Geary, Gur, Heyde, and Gernsbacher, "Sex, Math and Scientific Achievement," *Scientific American*, November 28, 2007, 46–51.

6. Robert Plomin et al., "Genetic Influence on Long Delay in Two-Year-Old Children," *Nature Neuroscience* 1, no. 4 (1998): 324–28.

7. The classic book on this topic is Deborah Tannen, *You Just Don't Understand: Women and Men in Conversation* (New York: William Morrow & Company, 1990).

8. Nikhil Swaminathan, "Gender Jabber: Do Women Talk More Than Men?" *Scientific American*, July 6, 2007.

9. Albert Mehrabian, a professor at the University of California, Los Angeles, has done this pioneering work on the importance of verbal and nonverbal messages.

10. "Fast Forces of Attraction," *Psychology Today*, January–February 2008.

11. Ibid.

12. See June Kronholz, "Talk Is Cheap in Politics, but a Deep Voice Helps," *Wall Street Journal*, November 3–4, 2007.

13. Richard B. Woodward, "Understanding Nixon from the Inside Out," *The Wall Street Journal*, May 10, 2007, available at http://online.wsj.com/articles/SB117875388193597871.html.

14. Deepak Malhotra and Max H. Bazerman, *Negotiation Genius: How to Overcome Obstacles and Achieve Brilliant Results at the Bargaining Table and Beyond* (New York: Bantam, 2007).

15. Daniel Goleman, "E-Mail Is Easy to Write (and to Misread)," *New York Times*, October 7, 2007.

16. Marcus Baram, "Fired Wal-Mart Exec Fires Back, Claims 'Smear Tactic,'" *ABC News*, March 29, 2007. Randall Stross, "How to Lose Your Job on Your Own Time," *New York Times*, December 30, 2007.

Chapter 5

1. Barbara Johnstone, "Community and Contest: Midwestern Men and Women Creating Their Worlds in Conversational Storytelling," *Gender*

and Conversational Interaction, ed. Deborah Tannen (New York: Oxford University Press, 1993, 62–80.

2. Dan P. McAdams, *The Redemptive Self: Stories Americans Live By* (City TK: Oxford University Press, 2006); Benedict Carey, "This Is Your Life (and How You Tell It)," *New York Times,* May 22, 2007.

3. Pauline R. Clance and Maureen A. O'Toole, "The Imposter Phenomenon: An Internal Barrier to Empowerment and Achievement," available at http://www2.gsu.edu/~wwwaow/resources/ip_internal_barrier_to_empwrmnt_and_achv.pdf.

5. Carey, "This Is Your Life (and How You Tell It)."

Chapter 6

1. Andrea Thompson, "Eyes Can't Resist Beautiful People," LiveScience .com.

2. This study, "Why Beauty Matters," was conducted by Markus Mobius of the Harvard economics department and Tanya Rosenblat of Wesleyan University. See the abstract at http://trosenblat.web.wesleyan .edu/home/beauty2005.pdf.

3. Dr. Daniel Hamermesh and Jeff E. Biddle conducted the research. See the study "Beauty and the Labor Market," http://ideas.repec.org/p/nbr/nberwo/4518.html.

4. J. Andreoni and R. Petrie, "Beauty, Gender and Stereotypes: Evidence from Laboratory Experiments," *Journal of Economic Psychology,* February 2008.

5. Roy F. Baumeister and Kristin L. Sommer, "What Do Men Want? Gender Differences and Two Spheres of Belongingness: Comment on Cross and Madson (1997)," *Psychological Bulletin* 122 (1997): 41; Jonathan Gottschall, "Greater Emphasis on Female Attractiveness in Homo Sapiens: A Revised Solution to an Old Evolutionary Riddle," *Evolutionary Psychology* (2007)5, no. 2: 347–57.

6. Malcolm Gladwell's popular book *Blink: The Power of Thinking Without Thinking* (Boston: Back Bay Books, 2007) is about the power of thin-slicing.

7. Ibid. New York University has done research on microthin-slicing; one study found that people make eleven decisions about other people in the first seven seconds. See also Robert Lee Hotz, "Some Scientists Argue We Are Built to Coo at the Sight of a Baby," *Wall Street Journal,* April 4, 2008, B1.

8. Cheryl Lu-Lien Tan, "The First Lady Sends Messages with Dresses," *The Wall Street Journal,* January 22, 2009, D1, 4.

9. See Amanda Christine Miller, "Arianna Embraces Her Femininity," What's My Logo? *Huffington Post,* April 7, 2008, www.huffingtonpost .com/amanda-christine-miller/emwhats-my-logoem-arianna_b_ 95337.html.

10. Christina Binkley, "Risky Business: Decolletage at a Work Dinner," *Wall Street Journal,* May 8, 2008, D10; and Christina Binkley, "The 'Sex Effect' on Office Dressing," *Wall Street Journal,* May 29, 2008, D10.

11. Dee Dee Myers, *Why Women Should Rule the World* (New York: Harper, 2008).

12. This research was done at the University of Bristol in England and is available at http://www.cs.bris.ac.uk/Publications/Papers/2000699 .pdf. Also see "Facial Attraction," *Allure,* June 2008.

13. Nikhil Swaminathan, "How Beauty Shapes Up Takes More Than a Good Build," *Scientific American,* March 13, 2007.

14. For the University of Utah flirting studies, see "Flirting on the Job," *Allure,* January 2008, 101.

Chapter 7

1. Alice H. Eagly and Linda L. Carli, *Through the Labyrinth: The Truth About How Women Become Leaders* (Boston: Harvard Business School Press, 2007); Alice H. Eagly and M. C. Johannesen-Schmidt, "Transformational, Transactional, and Laissez-Faire Leadership Styles: A Meta Analysis Comparing Women and Men," *Journal of Social Issues* 57: 781–97; "When the Boss Is a Woman," *Psychology Matters,* January 15, 2008.

2. See Eagly and Carli, *Through the Labyrinth.*

3. Ibid.

4. For more on the Kennedy School's Center for Public Leadership, see http://content.ksg.harvard.edu/leadership/.

5. Isabel Briggs Myers et al., *MBTI Manual* (Palo Alto: CPI, 1998) 157–158.

6. Ibid.

7. Alice H. Eagly, "Achieving Relational Authenticity in Leadership: Does Gender Matter?" *Leadership Quarterly* 16 (2005): 459–74.

8. Ibid.; Janet Shibley Hyde, "The Gender Similarities Hypothesis," *American Psychologist* 581 (September 2005): 581–92.

9. Alice Eagly, Northwestern University, e-mail exchanges with the author, summer 2008.

10. Alice Eagly used the word *androgynous* in our e-mail exchange on the subject.

11. See Erin White, "Art of Persuasion Becomes Key," *Wall Street Journal*, May 19, 2008, B5.

12. Roy F. Baumeister, "Is There Anything Good About Men?" address to the American Psychological Association, 2007.

13. Alan Feingold, "Gender Differences in Personality: A Meta-Analysis," *Psychological Bulletin* 116, no. 3 (November 1994): 420–56; Susan Pinker, *The Sexual Paradox: Men, Women and the Real Gender Gap* (New York: Scribner, 2008).

14. Catherine Hakim, *Work-Lifestyle Choices in the 21st Century: Preference Theory* (New York: Oxford University Press, 2000).

15. Lisa Belkin, "The Opt-Out Revolution," *New York Times*, October 26, 2003; Anne Preston, "Why Have All the Women Gone? A Study of Exit of Women from Science and Engineering Professions," *American Economic Review* 84, no. 5 (1994).

16. Daniel Kahneman, Alan B. Krueger, David A. Schkade, Norbert Schwarz, and Arthur A. Stone, "A Survey Method for Characterizing Daily Life Experience: The Day Reconstruction Method," *Science* 3, December 2004, vol. 306. no. 5702: 1776–80. Available at http://www .sciencemag.org/cgi/content/abstract/306/5702/1776.

17. Sylvia Martinez, "Women's Intrinsic and Extrinsic Motivations for Working," in *Being Together, Working Apart: Dual-Career Families and the Work-Life Balance*, ed. Barbara Schneider and Linda J. Waite (Cambridge: Cambridge University Press, 2005).

18. Lionel Tiger and Joseph Sepher, *Women in the Kibbutz* (New York: Harcourt, Brace, Jovanovich, 1975).

19. Nicholas D. Kristof, "Mistress of the Universe," *The New York Times*, February 8, 2009. See http://www.nytimes.com/2009/02/08/opinion/ 08kristof.html, which has links to the two studies.

20. Linda Babcock and Sara Lascheve, *Women Don't Ask: Negotiation and the Gender Divide* (Princeton: Princeton University Press, 2003).

Chapter 8

1. Simon Baron-Cohen, *The Essential Difference: Male and Female Brains and the Truth About Autism* (New York: Basic Books, 2004); Susan

Pinker, *The Sexual Paradox: Men, Women and the Real Gender Gap* (New York: Scribner, 2008).

2. Baumeister, "Is There Anything Good About Men?" address to the American Psychological Association, 2007.

3. Jared Sandberg, "People Can't Resist Doing a Big Favor—or Asking for One," *Wall Street Journal,* December 18, 2007, www.wsj.com.

4. Albright made this comment at the Women's National Basketball Association's "Celebrating Inspiration" luncheon, July 12, 2006. Mechelle Vopel, "Albright Empowers All-Decade Team at Luncheon," http://sports.espn.go.com/wnba/columns/story?id=2517642.

Chapter 9

1. David McCullough, *John Adams* (New York: Simon & Schuster, 2001). Quote available at http://en.wikiquote.org/wiki/John_Adams.

2. Catalyst, "2007 Catalyst Census of Women Corporate Officers and Top Earners of the Fortune 500," December 2007, www.catalyst.org/publication/13/2007-catalyst-census-of-women-corporate-officers-and-top-earners-of-the-fortune-500; and Rebecca R. Hastings, "Female Board Member Progress Differs in U.S. and U.K.," *SPHR,* December 2007.

3. Sue Shellenbarger, "How Stay-at-Home Moms Are Filling an Executive Niche," *Wall Street Journal,* April 30, 2008.

4. Kurt Kiener, "Your Taste in Music Is Shaped by the Crowd," *New Scientist,* February 9, 2006.

5. See "We Remember Bad Times Better Than Good," *Science News,* August 28, 2007.

6. The California Institute of Technology and Stanford Graduate School of Business conducted the wine test. See Stephen Shankland, "Study: $90 Wine Tastes Better Than the Same Wine at $10," http://news.cnet.com/8301-13580_3-9849949-39.html.

7. Sam Roberts, "For Young Earners in Big City, a Gap in Women's Favor," *New York Times,* August 3, 2007.

8. The idea of self-efficacy was first developed by Albert Bandura, a psychologist at Stanford University in the 1970s, and is now a central concept in social science. See Melinda Beck, "If at First You Don't Succeed, You're in Excellent Company," *Wall Street Journal,* April 29, 2008.

9. Julie Andrews, *Home, A Memoir of My Early Years* (New York: Hyperion, 2008), 85.

INDEX